Strictly according to the latest CBSE syllabus, examination pattern and NCERT Textbook

CORE Social Science Economics

Understanding Economic Development

Class 10

By

J.P. Goel

Associate Professor & Head Deptt. of Economics (Retd)

Hindu (P.G.) College, Sonepat (Haryana)

Formerly, Member Board of Studies in Economics

Maharishi Dayanand University, Rohtak (Haryana)

Mrs. Kaushal Goel

Former, PGT in Economics

Malviya Shiksha Sadan Sr. Sec. School,

Sonepat (Haryana)

GOYAL BROTHERS PRAKASHAN

GOYAL BROTHERS PRAKASHAN

EDUCATIONAL PUBLISHERS

Sales & Registered Office :

11/1903, Chuna Mandi, Paharganj, New Delhi - 110055
Post Box : 5720, Phones : 43551877 & 43561877
E-mail : info@goyal-books.com
Website : www.goyal-books.com

Administrative Office :

D-231, Sector 63, Noida-201301 (U.P.)
Phone : 0120-4655555

Showrooms :

Ahmedabad: Y-10, Dev Castle Complex Opp. Radhekrishan Villa, Jaymala-Govindwadi Road Isanpur, Ahmedabad–382 443 (Gujarat) **Tel : 09925004030**

Chennai : No. 50/39 Ground Floor, Five Furlong Road Guindy, Chennai–600 032 (Tamil Nadu) **Tel : 044-29530414, 044-29530874**

Guwahati : H. No. 69, KRB Road, Beside Bharalumukh SO Guwahati - 781009, **Phone : 0361-2967044** , **Email** : guwahati@goyal-books.com

Hyderabad : F-7/8/41, First Floor, Agarwal Chambers, 5-9-1121, King Kothi Road, Hyderabad - 500001 **Tele-fax : 23211332**

Kochi : Fair Heavens, H.No. 52-2783/A, Shine Road, Vytilla Emakulam - 682019 (Kerala) **Phone : 0484-2305288**

Kolkata : No. 203, 2nd Floor, Fomra Towers, 84-A, Acharya Jagdish Chandra Bose Road, Kolkata - 700014 **Phone : 033-22262683**

Bengaluru : 1681/5/4, Ground Floor, 3rd Main Ramamohanapuram, Bengaluru - 560 021, **Phone : 080-23320655**

Bhopal : Plot No. 203, Zone-II, M.P. Nagar, Bhopal-462 011 (M.P.), **Tele-fax : 0755-4271371**

Lucknow : B-318, Sector-B, Mahanagar, Opposite P.A.C Main Gate, Lucknow - 226 006, **Phone : 0522-2320841**

Patna : Ravi Kiran Apartment, Flat No. 2-A, Second floor, Near Water Pumping Station, Pani Tanki Lane, Pirmohani, Patna – 800003

Nagpur : Thakkar Villa, House No. 436 Joshiwadi, Sitabuldi, Nagpur – 440012 **Phone : 9823655077**

To buy our books online log on to www.goyal-books.com

Edition : 2023
Price : ₹ 140

Published & Printed by
Roshan Lal Goyal for Goyal Brothers Prakashan, New Delhi

PREFACE

Core Social Science – Economics for Class 10 has been revised strictly according to the latest syllabus and examination pattern prescribed by the CBSE and the latest NCERT book (Understanding Economic Development).

This book introduces students to a simplified view of the process of development in the Indian economy. The purpose of the book is to understand the economic life around us and also to think about what we would mean by economic development of people. We have used many examples and case studies to aid in conceptual clarity.

Salient Features of this Book :

- The **text matter is narrative as well as critical and extensively cover all the topics** for the CBSE Board Examination.
- **Simple, lucid, learner-friendly approach** has been adopted to make the lessons interesting and easy to understand.
- The lessons are designed to help the learners **to develop skills of comprehension, evaluation and an ability to analyse the matter given.**
- In discussing the themes, the text has been supplemented by **pictures, graphs, tables, charts, examples and case studies from a variety of sources.**
- Interesting and extra information have been added in boxes.
- Each topic in the lesson is followed by **Let's Recapitulate** (for quick revision of important points), **Glossary** (important terms and concepts have been explained), **Check Your Understanding** (questions for evaluation).
- **Exercises** at the end of every chapter have been **designed** as per the **latest pattern of questions asked in the CBSE Board Examination**. These contain **Objective Type Questions** (MCQ, fill in the blanks, matching, arranging in correct sequence, assertion and reasoning, etc.), and **Subjective Type Questions** (very short, short and long answer type questions).

It is hoped that the teachers and students would find this book useful.

Constructive suggestions from parents, pupil, teachers and educationists are welcome.

J.P. Goel
&
Kaushal Goel
C-131B, Sushant Lok Phase III
Sector 57, Gurugram 122003
(Haryana)
Mobile : 9810945659
e-mail : jpgoel03@gmail.com

CONTENTS

1 Development

OUTLINE OF THE CHAPTER

At the end of the chapter students will come to know about :

- Meaning of Development
- National Development
- Public Facilities and Sustainability of Development

1.1 MEANING OF DEVELOPMENT

Every individual and every nation aspire for development or progress. Here we first need to understand what does the development mean? We cannot answer this question in a single line or word because there are several aspects or dimensions of development.

All human beings set up their own goals based on their hopes and aspirations. They try to achieve them and set up the next higher goal. Similarly, nations assess the resources available and lay down goals, which can be achieved. They then, formulate policies so that standard of living of the people can be improved. Once a target as goal is achieved, the next higher goal is set for coming years.

Different people and their different Development goals

Different categories of people have different aspirations and goals regarding development for progress in life.

The aspirations and goals of some of the categories of people are given in Table 1.1 below.

Table 1.1 : Development Goals of Different Categories of People

S. No.	Categories of People	Development Goals/Aspirations
1.	Landless rural labourers	• More days of work • Better wages • Quality education to their children
2.	Large (rich) farmers	• Higher prices for their crops and hence high family income • Availability of cheap farm labour or other inputs • Settlement of children abroad
3.	A rural woman	• Economic independence • Better living conditions • Equal wage for equal work • Ornament/Jewellery

4.	A worker in a factory	•	Better wages
		•	Smaller working hours
		•	Other benefits such as free meals, entertainment facilities
		•	Fair treatment by the factory owner
5.	An industrialist	•	Better infrastructural facilities like transport, banking, communication, insurance, etc.
		•	Low tax rate
		•	Assured supply of raw material and electricity at reasonable prices
		•	Luxurious living
		•	High status in the society
6.	A maid servant	•	Higher salary
		•	Less work and good working conditions
		•	A bicycle to go to work
		•	A mobile set to talk
		•	Free meals
		•	Festival gifts
7.	A boy from a rich family	•	High living standard
		•	Complete freedom with no interference in his affairs
		•	An expensive personal car.
		•	Foreign tour
		•	Education from a reputed institution
8.	A girl from a rich family	•	Equal treatment and freedom as provided to her brother
		•	Economic and social freedom
		•	To go abroad for higher study
		•	An expensive mobile set

In the above table, we find that different people have different goals or aspirations. They wish to have things that are most important for them.

In fact, at times, two persons or groups of persons may desire things which are conflicting. A girl expects as much freedom and opportunity as her brother, and that he also shares in the household work. Her brother may not like this. Similarly, workers in a factory want higher wages and more facilities. But the industrialists may like to keep the wages and other facilities as low as possible.

This clearly indicates that the development (or progress) for one person may not be the development for others.

Three Important Things

- Different persons have different development goals.
- What may be development for one, may not be development for the other.
- Income is essential for development, but besides it, people also seek equal treatment, good health and security etc.

Income and other goals of individuals

From the above mentioned examples, you can see that most developmental goals aim towards earning more income. More and more income is always needed to fulfil consumption needs as well as to enhance comforts. Everyone aspires to make life comfortable. Basic needs are food, shelter and clothing. But beyond these, all individuals desire more.

Besides more money income there are also some other factors in social life. Individual self-respect and dignity are equally important to people. A person may not take up a manual job as he feels that it is below his dignity. A person always looks for freedom of work, social equality, good work environment, friendly atmosphere and so on. Therefore while choosing a job, people seek to meet more than one goal. They do not look only for money income but also see security of job, timings, work conditions and so on (Flow Chart 1.1).

Flow Chart 1.1 : Income and Other Goals

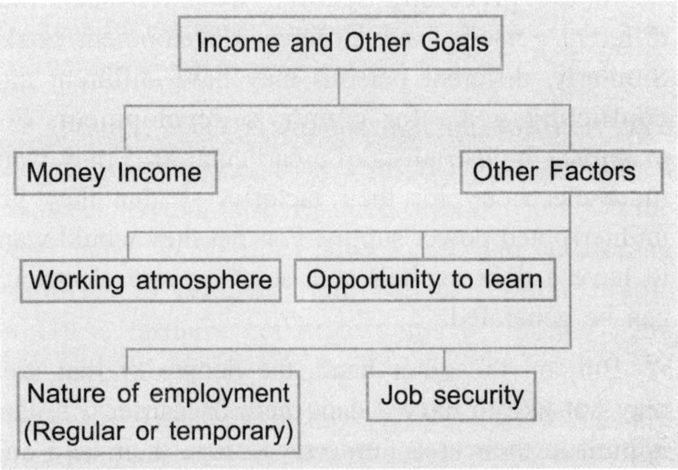

GLOSSARY

Development : In economics, development means the process by which the economic well-being and quality of life of a nation, region or local community are improved.

National Development : National development is the ability of a country to improve socio-ecomomic well being of its citizens.

Resources : An economic or productive factor required to accomplish an activity, or as means to undertake an enterprise and achieve desired outcome, for example, land, labour, capital, energy, entrepreneurship, information, expertise, management, etc.

Aspiration : A strong desire to achieve something high or great.

Economic freedom : The freedom to produce, trade and consume any goods and services acquired without the use of force, fraud or theft.

LET'S RECAPITULATE

- Every individual and every nation aspire for development as progress.
- All human beings set up their own goals based on their hopes and aspirations.
- Different categories of people have different aspirations and goals regarding development as they progress in life.
- At times, two persons or groups of persons may desire things which are conflicting.
- The development for one person may not be the development for others.
- Besides more money income, some other factors like, individual self-respect and dignity, etc., are equally important in social life.

CHECK YOUR UNDERSTANDING

1. Which of the following may be an aspiration for landless rural labourers?

(a) More days of work (b) Better wages

(c) Quality education to their children (d) All of these

2. Why do different persons have different development goals?

3. Explain how the aspirations (i.e. development goals) of a girl are different from those of a boy.

4. 'People may have conflicting goals'. Do you agree?

5. List some examples of goals other than income that are important in our social life.

1.2 NATIONAL DEVELOPMENT

In the preceding section, we have seen that different persons have different development goals. Similarly, different persons may have different and conflicting goals for country's development. For example : Industrialists of a particular area may want more electricity for their factories so that they get uninterrupted power supply. For that they would want to have a dam in their area so that more electricity can be generated.

But, on the other hand, the people of that area may not like to have a dam there. Because, if a dam is built in their area farmers will lose their land and livelihood. They will all have to shift from there. They will become homeless and jobless.

The villagers aspire for a sugar mill so that their sugarcane crops can be used to set up a sugar industry.

In both cases the goals aim at development, but they are at conflict. Building a dam may not only take away the possibility of setting up the sugar factory; it may even displace the villagers from that area.

Hence, the question arises that how can we synthesise between different goals. At the national level, the government has to see what goals need to be set so that maximum people could benefit from those goals.

How to Compare Different Countries or States?

How to compare different countries or states with regard to development? How can we say whether the development has taken place in a particular country or not? Or, how can we measure development or what are the indicators of development? The important indicators or measures of development are discussed below.

National Income

Nations and states are compared on the ground of **income** of people in that particular region. Each person earns an income for doing some production work. This income is directly related to the capacity of the people to spend and fulfil their immediate needs or goals. The total annual income of all people of the country is **'National Income'**.

- The level of development is indicated by the level of national income of the countries of the world.
- National income is the value of all final goods and services produced in a country during a year.
- Increase in income means more availability of goods and services to the people.
- Hence, increase in national income is regarded as an important development goal for a country.

Per Capita Income

- Per capita income means average national income i.e., per head national income. It can be obtained by dividing national income by the whole population.

$$\text{Per Capita Income} = \frac{\text{National Income}}{\text{Total Population}}$$

- National income alone cannot be considered as an indicator of development, especially in the case of those countries where the rate of population growth is higher than the rate of increase in national income. Hence, development should be measured in terms of per capita income. Increase in per capita income can only ensure availability of more goods and services per head. Hence, per capita income is considered as a better indicator of development compared to national income. However, per capita income cannot increase without the increase in national income. Therefore, in order to achieve higher level of development, every country tries to increase its national income as well as per capita income.

The World Bank classifies countries on the basis of per capita income.

- Countries with per capita income of US$ 12,056 per annum and above in 2017, are called rich countries.
- Countries with per capita income of US$ 955 or less are called low-income countries.
- India comes in the category of low middle income countries because its per capita income in 2017 was just US$ 1,820 per annum.

Why is per capita income of different countries calculated in dollars?

The per capita income of different countries is calculated in terms of US dollar. It is because of the fact that

- dollar is widely accepted currency of the world
- it ensures uniformity in calculation across different countries of the world.

Average income is undoubtedly useful for comparison but it does not tell us how income is distributed among people in a country, it may hide disparities. We can give an example to illustrate this fact clearly.

Suppose there are two countries : A and B, and only five citizens live in each country. Monthly income of the citizens living in both the countries are given in Table 1.2. On the basis of the data given in the table, we calculate average income of both the countries as under.

Table 1.2 : Comparison of Average Income of Two Countries (Monthly Income of Citizens)

Country	1	2	3	4	5	Total	Average
A	10,000	9,000	10,500	11,500	12,000	53,000	10,600
B	900	800	1,000	1,200	56,300	60,200	12,040

Even though the average income in country A is ₹10,600 while it is ₹ 12,040 in case of country B. If we see only average income, it is higher in country B. But country A is considered better as it has more equitable distribution of income.

In this country people are neither very rich nor extremely poor. On the other hand most citizens in country B are poor and one person is extremely rich. Hence, while average income is useful for comparison it does not tell us how this income is distributed among people.

Other Criteria as measures for development

Increase in national income and per capita income indicate development but these are not sufficient indicators. Besides higher level of income, people must also have basic amenities of life such as food, clothing, housing, health and education. Only then development can be of some use for the people of a country.

In this regard, a new concept of Human Development Index (HDI) was introduced since 1990 by the United Nations Development Programme (UNDP).

Human development is a process of widening people's choices as well as raising the well-being of people.

Table 1.3 : Some Data Regarding India and Its Neighbours for 2017

Countries	Gross National Income (GNI) Per Capita (2011 PPP $)	Life Expectancy at Birth (2017)	Mean Years of Schooling of People aged 25 and above (2017)	HDI Rank in the World (2018)
Sri Lanka	11,326	75.5	10.9	76
India	**6,353**	**68.8**	**6.4**	**130**
Myanmar	5,567	66.7	4.9	148
Pakistan	5,331	66.6	5.2	150
Nepal	2,471	70.6	4.9	149
Bangladesh	3,677	72.8	5.8	136

Source: Human Development Report, 2018, United Nations Development Programme, New York.

Human Development Index takes three aspects into account. It takes into account health, education and standard of living as the fundamental criteria for judgement of human development of a nation. It is a measure of average achievements in these three dimensions.

Isn't it surprising that a small country in our neighbourhood, Sri Lanka, is much ahead of India in every respect and a big country like ours has such a low rank in the world? Table 1.3 also shows that though Nepal and Bangladesh have low per capita income than that of India, yet they are better than India in life expectancy.

Steps Needed to Improve HDI

The following efforts should be made by any country to improve its HDI.

(i) Improving 100 per cent literacy to the people.
(ii) Improving health facilities.
(iii) Creating a pollution free environment.
(iv) Creating more and more productive employment opportunities.

Human Development Index

- Human Development Index (HDI) is an index that shows the level of human development in a nation.
- It is prepared by United Nations Development Programme annually.
- It measures human development by combining three indicators–Health, Education and Standard of living.
- Health is measured by life expectancy; educational achievement is measured by adult literacy rate and standard of living is measured by per capita income.
- The minimum and maximum values of HDI are measured on a scale between 0 and 1.

Comparison between States

Like nations, different states within the country, also vary in the levels of human development. Let us examine this point through an example of three states namely Haryana, Kerala and Bihar. Study Table 1.4 given below.

Table 1.4 : Comparative Data on Haryana, Kerala and Bihar

State	Per Capita Income for 2015-16 (in ₹)	Infant Mortality Rate (2016)	Literacy Rate (%) (2011)	Net Attendance Ratio (Per 100 person) secondary stage (age 14–15 years) (2013-14)
	(1)	(2)	(3)	(4)
Haryana	1,62,034	33	82	61
Kerala	1,40,190	10	94	83
Bihar	31,454	38	62	43

Sources: Economic Survey 2017-18, Vol. 2, Government of India, National Sample Survey Organisation (Report No. 575)

From the information given in Table 1.4, we find that

- Out of the three states Haryana (₹1,62,034) has the highest per capita income and Bihar (₹31,454) has the lowest per capita income.
- So, if per capita income were used as the measure of development, Haryana will be considered the most developed and Bihar the least developed state of the three.
- The second column of the table shows that in Kerala, out of 1,000 children born, 10 die before completing the one year of age. But in Haryana, this figure is 33 which is 3 times more than Kerala.
- Now also look at Column (3) of the table which shows the literacy rate. Kerala has the highest literacy rate at 94% which is much more when compared to Haryana and Bihar.
- Kerala has a Low infant mortality rate and a high literacy rate because it lays emphasis on human development.
- Last column of Table 1.4 shows around half of the children aged 14-15 years in Bihar are not attending school beyond Class 8.
- So income by itself is not a completely adequate indicator of development. Money alone cannot provide all the things that we need to live well. Therefore, while comparing different regions, apart from income, we should take care of some other criteria also. In order to raise the level of development we have to make provisions for many things.

Features of Human Development

- It is a broader concept of development as it includes health and educational aspects also along with per capita income.
- It puts human welfare at the centre of all other criteria.
- It focusses on the qualitative improvement of human life.
- Income is important but not an end in itself. It is a means to achieve human development.

GLOSSARY

Infant Mortality Rate (IMR) : It indicates the number of children that die before the age of one year as a proportion of 1,000 live children born in that particular year.

Mean years of schooling : It is an average number of years of education received by people over 18 years of age.

Per capita income : It means average national income of a country. It is calculated in dollars for all countries to make the data comparable.

National Income : National income is the total income of the residents of a country in a year.

Life expectancy at birth : Number of years a new born infant is expected to live.

Literacy rate : It measures the proportion of literate population in the 7 and above age group.

Net Attendance Ratio : *It is the total number of children of age group 14–15 years attending school as a percentage of total number of children in the same age group.*

LET'S RECAPITULATE

- At the national level, the government has to see what goals need to be set so that maximum people could benefit from those goals.
- Nations and states are compared on the ground of the income of people in that particular region.
- The level of development is indicated by the level of national income of the country.
- Per capita income is considered as a better indicator of development compared to national income.
- Besides higher level of income, people must also have basic amenities of life such as food, clothing, housing, health and education.
- A new concept of Human Development Index was introduced since 1990 by the United Nations Development Programme. It takes three aspects (namely per capita income, health and education) into account.
- Like nations, different states within the country, also vary in the level of human development.

CHECK YOUR UNDERSTANDING

1. How is per capita income calculated?
2. What is the basis on which World Bank has classified different countries?
3. 'Income alone cannot become an indicator of development'. Do you agree?
4. What is human development?
5. What are the aspects which are taken into account by United Nations for calculating Human Development Index?
6. Human development is a broader concept compared to economic development. Explain.
7. What does Human Development Index include?
8. What is Infant Mortality Rate?

1.3 PUBLIC FACILITIES AND SUSTAINABILITY OF DEVELOPMENT

Money in your pocket cannot purchase all the goods and services that you may need to live well. So, income by itself is not a complete and adequate indicator of material goods and services that citizens use. For example, normally, your money cannot purchase you a pollution-free environment or ensure that you get unadulterated medicines. Money may also not be able to protect you from infectious diseases, unless the whole of our community takes preventive steps.

Thus, public facilities need to be created by the government. The government plays an important role in providing amenities to people for their improved life. Some of these amenities include public transport, supply of water and electricity, government schools, colleges, hospitals and health centres, etc.

Kerala has a low Infant Mortality Rate (IMR) because it has adequate provision of basic health and educational facilities. Similarly, in some states, the Public Distribution System (PDS) functions well. For example, more people in Tamil Nadu get ration from ration shops through PDS at cheaper rates and of better quality as compared to othe states. Health and nutritional status of people of such states is certainly likely to be better.

Meaning of Sustainable Development

Over the last few years, the economists have put forward a new concept of economic development, i.e., **Sustainable Development**.

Sustainable development is the development which meets the needs of the present generation without harming the ability of future generation to meet their own needs. In this regard, we have to understand that environment and economy are inter-dependent. Hence the process of development should not ignore environmental issues. The development which ignores the environmental issues cannot be sustained. Hence, the sustainability of environment is the pre-condition for sustainable development.

Environment Problems

Rapid industrialisation and economic growth of the world in the past have led to several environmental problems. It has put a huge strain on limited natural resources on one hand and has polluted the environment on the other. Overuse and misuse of resources have led to environmental issues.

- **Overuse of Resources :** It implies excessive use of natural resources.

  Examples :

  (a) Excessive extraction of minerals

  (b) Excessive use of groundwater for irrigation

- **Misuse of Resources :** It implies irrational use of resources. That is, diversion of resources to use which cause environmental degradation.

Examples :

(a) Use of rivers to absorb industrial waste

(b) Falling of trees to get wood for fuel

Concept of Sustainable Development

Sustainable development is an issue that has emerged from rapid industrialisation of the world in the past century. The fast development has put huge strain on our limited natural resources on one hand and has polluted the environment on the other. This kind of development seems to be unsustainable. In view of this fact, the concept of sustainable development was first propounded by **World Commision on Environment and Development** in its report submitted in 1987. World Commission on Environment and Development was set up by the United Nations. The commission is also known as Brundtland Commission named after its Chairman Harlem Brundtland.

Features of Sustainable Development

Sustainable development has the following main features :

(1) Present and Future Generations : Sustainable development puts emphasis on the welfare of both present generation and future generation.

(2) Emphasis on Equality : It lays emphasis both on inter-generational and intra-generational equity. This concept is based on principles of equity and social justice. Thus, it requires all generations, present as well as future to make the best use of their potential capabilities.

(3) Rational Use of Natural Resources : Sustainable development emphasises the need for rational use of natural resources. To achieve long term well-being, they should not be excessively utilised. It aims at making use of natural resources and environment for raising the present standard of living in such a way as not to reduce the ability of future generations.

(4) Environmental Protection : It emphasises that the cost of development, particularly environmental cost should be taken into account. It, thus, stresses upon the need for the protection of environment.

Renewable and Non-renewable Resources

Natural resources can be classified as (i) renewable resources and (ii) non-renewable resources.

- Renewable resources refer to those resources which are not exhausted or depleted on use. Forests, sea animals, water, sunshine, etc., are included in this category.

- Non-renewable resources are those resources which are exhausted or depleted on use. These are available to us from nature as a fixed stock. Once exhausted, we will have to find substitute for them. Coal, crude oil, etc., are some examples of non-renewable resources. Middle East has the largest crude oil reserves.

How can Sustainable Development be Achieved?

To achieve sustainable development the following factors needs to be done :

(i) Avoidance of overuse of resources.

(ii) Renewable resources should be extracted on a sustainable basis. In other words, the rate of extraction should not exceed the rate of regeneration.

(iii) The rate of depletion of non-renewable resources should not exceed the rate of growth of renewable substitutes.

GLOSSARY

Public facilities : These are the services provided by the government to its citizens, e.g., infrastructure, sanitation, public transport, health care, water, etc.

Unadulterated : Something that is pure and not mixed with other ingredients.

Public distribution system : It is a government-sponsored chain of shops entrusted with the work of distributing basic food and non-food commodities to the needy sections of the society at very cheap prices.

Sustainable development : It can be defined as development that meets the needs of the present without compromising the ability of future generations to meet their own needs.

Natural resources : A natural resource is what people can use which comes from the natural environment, e.g., air, water, wood, oil, wind energy, natural gas, iron, coal, etc.

Environment : The surroundings or conditions in which a person, animal, or plant lives or operates.

LET'S RECAPITULATE

- Income by itself is not a complete and adequate indicator of material goods and services that citizens use.
- The government plays an important role in providing amenities to people for their improved life.
- Kerala has a low infant mortality rate because it has adequate provision of basic health and educational facilities.
- Sustainable development is the development which meets the needs of the present generation without harming the ability of future generation to meet their own needs.
- Main features of sustainable development are, emphasis on equality, rational use of natural resources, environmental protection, care for present and future generations etc.

CHECK YOUR UNDERSTANDING

1. Which of the following states has low infant mortality rate?
   (a) Kerala (b) Madhya Pradesh (c) Punjab (d) Andhra Pradesh
2. Why should the government open schools and hospitals?
3. Define sustainable development.
4. Who coined the concept of sustainable development?
5. 'Sustainable development is directly related to the rational utilisation of natural resources'. Explain.

EXERCISES

I. A. Multiple choice questions.

1. Which of the following is most likely to be a development goal for landless rural labourers? [CBSE 2010]
   (a) Highest support prices for their crops
   (b) They should be able to settle their children abroad
   (c) Raised wages
   (d) None of these
2. Which of the following is most important component for comparing different countries? [CBSE 2010]
   (a) Population (b) Income (c) Per capita income (d) Education
3. GDP is the total value of ____________ produced. [CBSE 2011]
   (a) all goods and services (b) all final goods and services
   (c) all intermediate goods and services (d) all intermediate and final goods and services
4. Development goals of different sections of our society can be achieved by [CBSE 2011]
   (a) force (b) democratic political process
   (c) violent agitation (d) terrorism
5. If there are five persons in a family and their total income is ₹ 20,000. What would be the average income of each person? [CBSE 2011]
   (a) ₹ 6,000 (b) ₹ 4,000 (c) ₹ 5,000 (d) ₹ 10,000
6. What does Infant Mortality Rate indicate?
   (a) Literate population in the seven and above age
   (b) The number of children that die before the age of one year as proportion of 1000 live children
   (c) The total number of children attending the school
   (d) The number of children born in a year
7. Suppose, in country X, 10,00,000 children were born in the year 2009. Out of these 90,000 died between age of 1 and 5 years and 60,000 died before 1 year of age. Infant Mortality Rate per 1,000 children will be [CBSE 2011]
   (a) 90 (b) 60 (c) 30 (d) 80
8. "Kerala has low infant mortality rate". Which of the following is appropriate reason for the same? [CBSE 2010]
   (a) It has adequate provision of basic health and educational facilities.
   (b) It has highest per capita income.
   (c) It has natural resources.
   (d) The Government of Kerala is very efficient.
9. Human Development Index was introduced since
   (a) 1947 (b) 1951 (c) 1990 (d) 2001
10. Human development emphasises on
    (a) welfare of the people (b) income of the people
    (c) equitable distribution of income (d) protection of environment
11. Human Development Report is published by [CBSE 2011]
    (a) UNDP (b) World Bank (c) IMF (d) WHO
12. Which of the following is not a component of Human Development Index? [CBSE 2011]
    (a) Life expectations (b) Gross enrollment ratio (c) Per capita income (d) National income
13. Which of the following has the largest crude oil reserves?
    (a) USA (b) Russia (c) China (d) The middle east
14. Which of the following countries has higher HDI rank than India? [CBSE 2011]
    (a) Sri Lanka (b) Nepal (c) Bangladesh (d) Pakistan

B. Fill in the blanks.

1. The number of deaths of children less than one year of age per 1,000 live births is referred as ________________. [CBSE Sample Question Paper 2019-20]
2. ____________________ indicates the place of the countries in relation to other countries in the field of human development.
3. Different people have different ________________.
4. The main drawback of per capita income as an indicator of development is that it ignores the distribution of ________________.
5. Groundwater is a ____________________ resource.
6. One of the best ways to reduce over-usage of groundwater is ____________________. [CBSE Sample Question Paper 2019-20]
7. The total number of children of age group 14–15 years attending school as a percentage of total number of children in the same age group is referred to as ___________. [CBSE Sample Question Paper 2019-20]

C. In the question given below, there are two statements marked as Assertion (A) and Reason (R). Read the statements and choose the correct option. [CBSE Sample Question Paper 2019-20]

Assertion (A) : Not every good or service that is produced and sold needs to be counted to know the total production in each sector.

Reason (R) : The value of final goods already includes the value of all the intermediate goods.

Options :

(a) Both A and R are true and R is the correct explanation of A.
(b) Both A and R are true but R is not the correct explanation of A.
(c) A is correct but R is wrong.
(d) A is wrong but R is correct.

D. Choose the incorrect option from the following statements.

Which of the following statement defines Sustainable Development? [CBSE Sample Question Paper 2019-20]

(a) Sustainable use of natural resources without considering the need of the future generation.
(b) Present generation fulfils its needs while considering the needs of the future generations as well.
(c) It means utilisation of natural resources by the past, present and forthcoming future generation.
(d) To meet the needs of the future generations even if the needs of the present generation go unmet.

E. Match the following terms given in Column A with those in Column B. Choose the correct answer from the options given below.

	Column A		Column B
A.	Total annual income of all people of the countries	(i)	Per capita income
B.	National Income/Total Population	(ii)	National income
C.	Human Development Index	(iii)	Emphasis on human welfare
D.	Standard of Living	(iv)	United Nations Development Programme

Mark the correct option.

(a) A-(i), B-(iii), C-(iv), D-(ii)
(b) A-(ii), B-(iii), C-(i), D-(iv)
(c) A-(ii), B-(i), C-(iv), D-(iii)
(d) A-(iii), B-(ii), C-(i), D-(iv)

II. A. Very short answer type questions.

1. Mention any two developmental goals of landless labourer.
2. Mention any two developmental goals of girl child belonging to a rich family.
3. What do you understand by national income?
4. Define GDP. [CBSE 2015]
5. What is meant by national income? [CBSE 2017]
6. How do we calculate per capita income of the countries? [CBSE 2015]

7. On what basis has the World Bank classified countries into rich, middle and poor income countries?
8. Which countries according to World Bank are called rich countries? [CBSE 2017]
9. In which income category does India fall as per the World Bank?
10. Why is per capita income regarded a better indicator of development compared to national income?
11. What is the main drawback of average income as a measure of development?
12. What is the sustainable development?
13. What is net attendance ratio?
14. Why has Kerala a low infant mortality rate?
15. Write the full form of HDI?
16. What is meant by human development?
17. What is infant mortality rate? [CBSE 2015]
18. In which state of India is the infant mortality rate lowest? [CBSE 2015]

B. Short answer type questions.

1. Name any three characteristics of development. [CBSE 2015]
2. What may be development for one may not be development for the other. Explain with the help of examples.
3. Different categories of persons have different developmental goals. Explain it with any two examples.
4. Give some examples where factors other than income are important aspect of our lives.
5. Define per capita income. How is it calculated? [CBSE 2011, 2016]
6. Why is average income regarded as an important criterion for development? Explain.
7. State any two goals of development other than income.
8. How can two persons have different developmental goals?
9. Why do people look for a mix of goals for development?
10. Do you think money in your pocket can buy all the goods and services you may need to live well? Support your answer on four points. [CBSE 2015]

    Or

    "Money cannot buy all the goods and services that a person may need to live well." Explain the statement with suitable examples. [CBSE 2016]
11. Why should the public utilities be developed in a country?
12. Explain the concept of human development.
13. Explain the concept of sustainable development.
14. Why is the issue of sustainability important for development?
15. The average income in Haryana is more than that of Kerala but lags behind in literacy rate. Explain how a country can improve its HDI rank?
16. Differentiate between UNDP Report and World Bank Report. Why in UNDP report more reliable of the two? [CBSE 2015]
17. Which three efforts should be made by any country to improve its HDI. [CBSE 2015]

C. Long answer type questions.

1. What is meant by economic development? What are the two basis of measuring economic development of a country? [CBSE 2016]
2. In what respects is the criterion used by the UNDP for measuring development different from the one used by the World Bank? Explain. [CBSE 2011, 2015, 2016]
3. Differentiate between :

    (a) National income and per capita income

    (b) Renewable resources and non-renewable resources

4. What is an average income? What is its importance? Describe its limitations related to development. [CBSE 2016]

OR

Why do we use averages? Are there any limitations to their use? Illustrate with your own examples related to development. [CBSE 2016]

5. What lessons can you draw about the importance of income from the fact that Kerala, with lower per capita income, has a better human development ranking than Haryana?
6. Assume that there are only three families each in two countries A and B. Monthly income of these families is given in the following table From the table we see that they have same average income. Now explain which country is better off and why?

Country	Monthly Income of Families (in ₹)			Average Income (₹)
	I	II	III	
A	9,000	10,000	11,000	10,000
B	1,000	900	28,100	10,000

7. Explain the following statements :
   (a) People have different developmental goals.
   (b) People have conflicting developmental goals.
8. Explain the components of Human Development Index.
9. Why is sustainable development essential for economic growth? Give two reasons. [CBSE 2017]

OR

What is sustainable development? Why is the issue of sustainability important for development? Explain. [CBSE 2018]

10. What is meant by sustainable development? Write its main features. [CBSE 2016]
11. Suggest measures for sustainable development.
12. What is sustainable economic development? Write any three measures to control environmental degradation.
13. What indicators are used in Human Development Index to measure the development of a country? [CBSE 2015]
14. What is Human Development Index? What are its basic components? [CBSE 2016]

ANSWERS

MCQS

1. (c) 2. (c) 3. (b) 4. (b) 5. (b) 6. (b) 7. (b) 8. (a)
9. (c) 10. (a) 11. (a) 12. (b) 13. (d) 14. (a)

Fill in the blanks

1. Infant mortality rate
2. HDI
3. Development goals
4. Income
5. Renewable
6. Harvesting of rainwater
7. Secondary education enrolment ratio

2

Sectors of the Indian Economy

OUTLINE OF THE CHAPTER

At the end of the chapter students will come to know about :

- Sectors of Economic Activities
- Where are Most of the People Employed?
- Division of Sectors

2.1 SECTORS OF ECONOMIC ACTIVITIES

When we look around us, we find that different people are engaged in different types of economic activities to earn their livelihood. A farmer ploughs his field, a weaver spins yarn and weaves cloth, a labourer works in a factory, a shopkeeper sells his goods on his shop, a computer operator or a clerk works in his office, a teacher teaches in school, a doctor treats patients in the hospital, etc. They all work to earn income with a view to satisfy their wants. All such economic activities form the basis of an economy.

Some of these activities produce goods while others are producing services. To understand these activities, we classify them into broad groups. These groups are called sectors of an economy. This chapter discusses the various sectors of the Indian economy.

On the basis of nature of economic activities, an economy is broadly classified into three main sectors, i.e., primary sector, secondary sector and tertiary sector (or service sector).

Primary Sector

In this sector of the economy, goods are produced by exploiting economy's natural resources. For example, nature has a great hand in the production of agricultural commodities. Likewise, nature cooperates with man in producing wood or timber, in raising cattle or in catching fish. Goods produced by this sector are known as *primary goods* or *natural products*. Primary sector is also known as **agricultural sector and related sector.**

*When we produce a good by exploiting natural resources, it is an activity of the **primary sector**. This is primary because it forms the base for all other products that we produce.*

Secondary Sector

Secondary sector includes all those activities which produce goods with the help of raw material produced in the primary sector. Since this sector is associated with different kinds of industries it is called **industrial sector**. Goods produced by this sector are known as *manufactured goods* or *secondary goods.*

Here primary products (or natural products) are converted into finished goods through the process of manufacturing. This could be in a factory or a workshop or at home. For example, using cotton fibre from the plant, we spun yarn and weave cloth; using wheat as raw material, we make flour and bread; using sugarcane we make sugar or gur (*Jaggery*).

Tertiary Sector

It is the third sector of the Indian economy. ***Tertiary means third in order***. It does not produce goods (as produced by the primary and secondary sectors). The activities of this sector help in the development of primary and secondary sectors.

For example, goods produced in the primary or secondary sector would need to be transported by trucks or trains and then sold in wholesale and retail shops. At times, it may be necessary to store these in godowns. We also may need to talk to others over telephone or send letters (communication) or borrow money from banks (banking) to help production and sale of goods.

Transport, communication, trade, banking, insurance and all other business services are the examples of tertiary services.

Interdependence between the Three Sectors

Though economic activities are grouped into three different sectors, they are highly interdependent and complementary to each other. The development of one sector depends on the other. For example, the primary sector (mainly agricultural sector) gets many agricultural inputs such as fertilisers, pesticides, pump sets, tractors, etc., from the secondary sector. And the secondary sector (mainly industrial sector) also gets supply of raw materials such as cotton, jute, sugarcane, oilseeds, wool, etc., from the primary sector.

Similarly, both the primary and secondary sectors depend on the tertiary sector for services such as transport and communication services, banking and insurance facilities, etc. In its turn, tertiary sector also depends on the primary sector for food and on the secondary sector for supply of computers, calculators, trucks, stationery, etc.

Comparing the three sectors

The various production activities in all the three sectors produce a very large number of goods and services. Now two questions arise :

(i) What is the contribution of these sectors in the production of total goods and services of the economy?

(ii) How do we count the value of various goods and services produced in each sector?

Regarding the first question, thousands of goods and services are produced in an economy. All goods are measured differently in physical terms. For example, wheat is expressed in kilograms or quintals, milk in litres and cloth in metres. It is an impossible task to add up the physical quantities of all these goods.

In order to solve this problem, we take the market value of all these goods and services with their respective market prices. For instance, if 50 quintals of wheat are produced in the agricultural sector and the price of wheat is ₹1,000 per quintal, the market value of wheat will be ₹50,000. The value of 1,000 metres of cloth at ₹20 per metre will be ₹20,000. Similarly the value of goods and services in the three sectors are calculated, and then added up.

We now take up the second question. Regarding this we need to understand the meanings of intermediate goods and final goods clearly.

Intermediate Goods

Intermediate goods are those producer goods which are used by the producers in the process of production. For example, a farmer uses seeds, fertilisers, water etc. to produce wheat; a carpenter uses wood to produce/manufacture furniture; a publisher buys paper for the production of books. All these goods are intermediate goods. Cars purchased by a car dealer from the company are also intermediate goods becuase they are meant for resale. *Thus intermediate goods are sold by one producer to another either for further processing or for resale.*

Final Goods

Final goods are sold to final users. They are neither meant for further processing nor meant for resale.

Let us take an example to illustrate it. Suppose a farmer produces cotton and sell it to spinning mill. Then spinning mill converts cotton to yarn and sells it to cloth mill. Then cloth mill converts yarn into cloth and sells it to garment manufacturer. The garment manufacturer produces ready made garments (say, shirts) and sells them to the consumers. Here in this example, shirts are the final goods. All other goods like cotton, cotton yarn and cloth are intermediate goods.

Airconditioners, refrigerators, washing machines and books are other examples of final goods.

The value of final goods and services produced in each sector during a particular year provides the total production of the sector for that year. And the sum of production in the three sectors gives what is called the **Gross Domestic Product (GDP)** of a country. It is the value of all final goods and services produced within a country during a particular year.

Why do we include the value of final goods only?

Intermediate goods are not included while estimating country's gross domestic product. The reason being the intermediate goods are used up in producing final goods and services. The value of final goods already includes the value of all intermediate goods that are used in making the final goods. This can be illustrated with the help of an example.

Example :

- Suppose, a farmer produces wheat and sells it to miller for ₹2,000.
- The miller purchases wheat and sells flour to the baker for ₹3,000.
- The baker converts the flour into bread and sells it to the retailer for ₹4,500.
- Then, the retailer sells the entire stock of bread to the final consumers for ₹6,000.

If we take, the value of goods of all the producers, it comes to ₹15,500 as under :

Value of goods = 2,000 + 3,000 + 4,500 + 6,000 = ₹15,500

In this example, *bread is a final good. It includes the value of intermediate goods. Bread is sold to its final users. Only the value of bread will be counted.* If we take the value of all goods, then the value of wheat is counted four times, the value of flour three times and the value of bread twice.

Change in the relative importance of different sectors or historical change in sectors

Now we look into the changes that have taken place regarding the importance of different sectors in the economy.

- In the initial stages of development, primary sector was the dominating sector of the economy.
- As the methods of farming changed, it raised the production of agricultural goods. Agriculture sector began to prosper. Many people could now take up other occupations. Some people started migrating to the manufacturing sector. As the development took place, new methods of manufacturing were introduced. Now workers began to shift from farm to factories.
- As a result, the number of industrial workers increased substantially. Now people could enjoy more goods at cheaper rates. Secondary sector gradually became the most important in total production and employment.
- In the last few decades, there was further shift from secondary sector to tertiary sector. Now, there was greater demand for services like transportation, communication, education, health care and tourism. A large number of people of developed countries are now working in the service sector. The service sector has become the most important sector in terms of total production and employment.

Importance of different sectors in the indian economy

Before we discuss the relative importance of the three different sectors in the Indian economy, we need to understand the meaning of Gross Domestic Product (GDP).

- GDP is defined as the market value of all the final goods and services produced in the domestic territory of a country in a year.
- It includes the value of all final goods and services produced within the domestic territory of the country. These goods are produced both by resident as well as non-resident producers (e.g., multinational companies, foreign banks, etc.) within the domestic territories of the country. Gross domestic product includes the market value of the final goods and services produced by all such producers.

Let us now see how much each sector contributes to Indian economy i.e. share in total production or GDP.

Share in Total Production or GDP

The share of different sectors in the country's GDP is called sector composition.

Graph 1 : GDP by Primary, Secondary and Tertiary Sectors

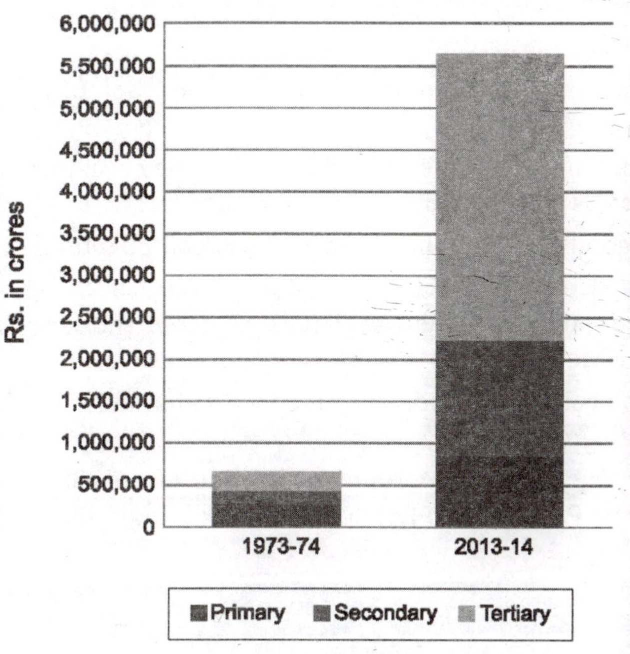

Graph 2.1 shows the production of goods and services in the three sectors. This is shown for two years, 1973-74 and 2013-14. You can see how the total production has grown over the 40 years.

Table 2.1 shows the share of different sectors in the total production of final goods and services, i.e., GDP during the period (1973-74 to 2013-14).

Table 2.1 : Percentage Share of Different Sectors in India's GDP

Sectors	1973	2007	2014
Primary	40%	19.8%	13%
Secondary	12%	24.5%	20%
Service	48%	55.7%	67%

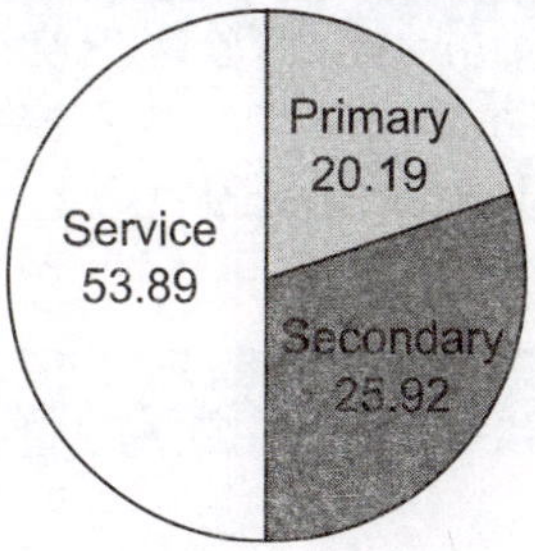

Fig. 2.1 : Percentage Share of Different Sectors in India's GDP in 2021

The given table clearly shows that during the period 1973-2014 the percentage share of primary sector in India's GDP has fallen whereas the percentage share of secondary and tertiary (service) sectors has increased.

In 2021 service sector is still the leading sector contributing 53.89% to GDP followed by secondary sector (25.92%) and primary sector (20.19%).

The tertiary sector (or the service sector) has emerged as the largest producing sector in India replacing the primary sector.

Factors responsible for the rising importance of tertiary sector

The main factors responsible for the growth of tertiary sector in India are as follows :

1. **Growth of Basic Services :** In any country several services such as hospitals, educational institutions, post and telegraph services, police stations, courts, village administrative offices, municipal corporations, defence, transport, banks, insurance companies, etc., are required. In a developing country, the government has to take responsibility for the provision of these basic services.
2. **Growth of Support Services :** The development of agricultural and industrial sectors requires several support services such as transport, trade, storage, banking, communication, etc. Hence in our country, with the development of agricultural and industrial sectors, the service sector has also expanded.
3. **Increase in Demand for Services :** Over the past four decades, income of people is rising. As income levels rise, the demand for services like eating out, shopping, tourism, private schools, professional training, etc., has increased.
4. **Demand for New services :** With modernisation and globalisation, some new services based on information technology and IT (Information Technology) enabled services have become important and essential. The production of these services has been rising rapidly.

GLOSSARY

Economic activity : Any action that involves producing, distributing, or consuming products or services, involving money or the exchange of products or services is called economic activity.

Primary activity : An activity related to the production of natural products, e.g., production of cotton and sugarcane.

Secondary activity : An activity which converts primary products into finished product through the process of manufacturing, e.g., sugar from sugarcane.

Tertiary activity : An activity that provides support service to primary and secondary sectors e.g., transportation of goods produced by primary and secondary sectors.

Intermediate goods : Intermediate goods are the goods used as raw materials in the production of other goods including final goods.

Final goods : Any commodity which is produced and subsequently consumed by the consumer, to satisfy his current wants or needs, is a consumer good or final good.

Retailer : A person or business that sells goods to the public in relatively small quantities for use or consumption rather than for resale.

GDP : Gross Domestic Product (GDP) is the monetary value of all finished goods and services made within a country during a specific period.

Domestic territory : Domestic territory is the geographical territory, administered by a government within which persons, goods and capital circulate freely.

Sector composition : Sector composition of an economy is the proportionate contribution of different sectors to the total Gross Domestic Product (GDP) of an economy during a year.

LET'S RECAPITULATE

- Different people are engaged in different types of economic activities to earn their livelihood.
- On the basis of the nature of economic activities, an economy is broadly classified into three main sectors.
- In the primary sector, goods are produced by exploiting economy's natural resources and it provides the base for all other products that we produce.
- In the secondary sector or industrial sector, primary products are converted into finished goods through the process of manufacturing.
- The tertiary sector helps in the development of primary and secondary sectors by providing various services like transport, communication, trade, banking, insurance, etc.
- The three sectors are highly interdependent and complementary to each other.
- Intermediate goods are sold by one producer to another either for further processing or for resale.
- The value of final goods and services produced in each sector during a particular year provides the total production of the sector for that year.
- Total production of the three sectors gives the Gross Domestic Product (GDP) of a country.
- Now, the service sector or the tertiary sector has become the most important in terms of total production and employment.
- The main factors responsible for the growth of tertiary sector in India are, growth of basic services and support services, increase in demand for services and demand for new services, etc.
- The share of different sectors in the total employment of a country is called occupational structure of the country.

CHECK YOUR UNDERSTANDING

1. What is primary sector? Why is it called agricultural sector?
2. Why is secondary sector called the industrial sector?

3. Classify the following activities into primary, secondary and tertiary sector activities :
   (a) Growing sugarcane
   (b) Fishing
   (c) Using of cotton to convert yarn and fabric
   (d) Hair cutting
   (e) Getting milk from animal
   (f) Tailoring
   (g) Training
   (h) Moneylending
   (i) Beekeeping
4. Differentiate between intermediate goods and final goods using some examples.
5. Classify the following in the intermediate and final goods :
   (a) Mobile sets purchased by a mobile dealer
   (b) Car purchased by a household
   (c) Milk purchased by a tea stall
   (d) Cold drink purchased by a student from school canteen
   (e) Fuel purchased by Delhi Transport Corporation
   (f) Chalks and duster purchased by a school
   (g) Office furniture
6. What is meant by sectoral composition?
7. What is occupational structure?

2.2 WHERE ARE MOST OF THE PEOPLE EMPLOYED (OR SHARE OF DIFFERENT SECTORS IN TOTAL EMPLOYMENT)

The share of different sectors in the total employment of a country is called occupational structure of the country. The occupational structure shows how each sector contributes to total employment. The share of the three sectors in employment for the period 1972-2012 is shown in Table 2.2 (a) and Table 2.2 (b).

Table 2.2 (a) : Percentage Share of Different Sectors in Employment

Sectors	1972-73	2004-05	2011-12
Primary	74%	56.6%	49%
Secondary	11%	18.7%	24%
Tertiary	15%	24.7%	27%

Table 2.2 (b) : Percentage Share of Different Sectors in Employment

Sectors	2017	2018	2019
Primary	43.93	43.33	42.60
Secondary	24.86	24.95	25.12
Tertiary	31.21	31.72	32.28

The above table (2.2 a) shows that there has been substantial shift from farm workers to non-farm workers during 2011-12.

- In 1972-73, about 74% of workforce were engaged in primary sector and in 2011-12, this proportion has declined to 49%.
- The shares of secondary and tertiary sectors have increased from 11% to 24% and 15% to 27% respectively.
- From 2017-2019 there has been little shift across sectors in employment.
- The primary sector is still the largest sector in terms of employment. The other important sector is the tertiary sector whose share is 32.28% in employment.
- A notable fact about India is that while there has been a change in the share of the three sectors in GDP, a similar shift has not taken place in employment.
  (a) Why didn't a similar shift out of primary sector happen in case of employment? It is because not enough jobs could be created in the secondary and tertiary sectors.
  (b) Though industrial production went up by more than 9 times during the period, employment in the industry went up by around 3 times. Similarly, the production in the service sector rose by 14 times, employment in this sector rose around 5 times.

(c) This implies that our agriculture sector is overcrowded. More people are engaged in agriculture than are actually required. In other words, workers in agriculture sector are underemployed or disguisedly unemployed.

Disguised Unemployment

Indian economy is facing the problem of unemployment – both open unemployment and disguised unemployment. Under open unemployment, people are willing to work at existing wage rate but they fail to find work. Under disguised unemployment people are seen working but they are not contributing to production. In other words, more people are employed than are actually required.

Disguised unemployment is also called hidden unemployment as it is not visible. All persons seem to be working.

The problem of disguised unemployment can be explained with the help of an example. Suppose a farmer owns one hectare of land. He has a family of 10 members. All are working on the same family farm. All of them are working on the same farm because they don't find alternative employment elsewhere. Suppose, 6 workers are needed on the farm. In this case 4 workers are disguisedly 'unemployed'. In such a case, if surplus workers are removed from the farm, there is no loss of production.

This kind of underemployment (or disguised unemployment) is found in many sectors of our economy. For example, there are thousands of casual workers who are engaged as painters, plumbers, electricians, carpenters and repair persons in our economy. They are always in search of daily employment but do not find work everyday.

Similarly, there are number of people in the service sector who work as pushcart and street vendors. They spend the whole day but earn very little. Thus all such people are doing the present work because they do not have better employment opportunities.

How to create more employment

In India, we are facing the problems of open unemployment, underemployment, unemployment and disguised unemployment in every sector of the economy. Now, we can see some of the important measures that can be adopted to create more employment opportunities, particularly in our rural areas.

Following are the factors that led to create employment opportunities :

1. **Diversification of Agriculture :** Diversification of agriculture can play a key role in rural development, where agriculture is the main occupation of people where about 50% of our workers are employed. There is a need to diversify agriculture. Farmers should be encouraged to adopt pisciculture, horticulture, animal rearing, etc., along with cultivation of crops.

2. **Expansion of Irrigation Facilities :** In India, we have most unirrigated land which is capable of giving only one crop a year. Most of the agricultural employment opportunities in India are generated in the kharif period (the monsoon season). Our government needs to make sincere efforts to increase irrigation facilities. This would enable the farmers to grow more than one crop in a year. Thus we can provide employment to more people on the same land by just increasing irrigation facilities.

3. **Provision of Basic Facilities :** In India, rural areas lack basic facilities like transport, storage, banking facilities, etc. The government need to invest money in creating these facilities. This will create employment opportunities in the farm sector as well as in services like transport, trade, storage, etc.

4. **Provision of Local Industries and Services :** Another way by which we can tackle this problem is to identify, promote and locate industries and services in semi-rural areas where a large number of people may be employed. For example,

   - Setting up a *dal* mill can help the farmers who grow pulse crops.
   - Similarly, if a cold storage is constructed, it can provide opportunities to farmers to store their products like potatoes, onions, apples, oranges etc., and sell these when the price is good.
   - In villages near forest areas, we can start honey collection centres where farmers can come and sell wild honey.
   - Processing industries can also be set up to process vegetables, potatoes, rice, wheat, tomatoes, fruits, etc. Their products can be sold in towns and cities.

   All these activities can create lot of employment opportunities.

5. **Expansion of Education and Health Facilities:** There is a great scope for job creation in our education and health sectors. In India, about 60% of the population belongs to the age group 5-29 years. Out of this, only about 51% are attending educational institutions. By planning education for all in the country, we will require more school buildings and more teachers and other staff. It is estimated that nearly 20 lakh jobs can be created in the education sector alone. Similarly, if we want to improve the health of our people, we need more doctors, nurses and hospitals also.
6. **Tourism and Regional Craft Industries :** Every state or region has potential to create jobs for people in that area. Tourism has a big scope in this direction. It is estimated that if developed properly, tourism as a sector can provide additional employment to more than 35 lakh people every year.
7. **Creating Employment Opportunities in Urban Areas :** For creating employment opportunities in urban areas the following ways can be suggested.
   (i) Heavy investment in infrastructure.
   (ii) Reform in education system.
   (iii) Providing loans to people who want to start their business.

Mahatma Gandhi National Rural Employment Guarantee Act (MGNREGA)

In India the central government passed a law implementing the **Right to Work** in about 625 districts of India. It is called Mahatma Gandhi National Rural Employment Guarantee Act (MGNREGA) 2005.

Under this scheme, all those who are able to, and are in need of work in rural areas are guaranteed 100 days of employment in a year by the government. If the government fails in its duty to provide employment within 15 days of the demand for work, it will give unemployment allowances to those who have applied for work.

GLOSSARY

Occupational structure : It refers to the distribution or division of the population according to different occupations such as primary, secondary and tertiary.

Unemployment : It occurs when a person who is actively searching for employment is unable to find work.

Disguised Unemployment : Disguised unemployment or hidden unemployment is a kind of unemployment in which there are people who are visibly employed but are actually unemployed or more people are engaged in a work than required.

Underemployment : The condition in which people in a labourforce are employed at less than full-time or regular jobs or at jobs inadequate with respect to their training or economic needs.

LET'S RECAPITULATE

- The occupational structure shows how each sector contributes to total employment.
- During 2011-12, there has been substantial shift from farm workers to non-farm workers.
- Indian economy is facing the problem of unemployment – both open unemployment and disguised unemployment in every sector of the economy.
- Some of the important measures that can be adopted to create more employment, particularly in rural areas are as follows :
  (i) Diversification of agriculture
  (ii) Expansion of irrigation facilities
  (iii) Provision of basic facilities
  (iv) Provision of local industries and services
  (v) Expansion of education and health facilities
  (vi) Tourism and regional craft industries
- Mahatma Gandhi National Rural Employment Guarantee Act was passed in the year 2005.

CHECK YOUR UNDERSTANDING

1. Why do you think MGNREGA 2005 is referred to as 'Right to work'?
2. Imagine that you are the village head. In that capacity suggest some activities that you think should be taken up under this Act that would also increase the income of people? Discuss.
3. How would income and employment increase if farmers were provided with irrigation and marketing facilities?
4. In what ways can employment be increased in urban areas?

2.3 DIVISION OF SECTORS

On the basis of terms and conditions of employment, economic activities can be divided into organised and unorganised sectors.

Organised Sector

Organised sector covers those enterprises or places of work where there are rules and regulations of work. Workers of organised sector get regular and assured employment. The enterprises of this sector are registered by the government and they have to obey government rules and regulations which are mentioned in various laws such as Factories Act, Minimum Wages Act, Payment of Gratuity Act, Shops and Establishment Act. It is called organised because it has some formal processes and procedures. That is why, it is sometimes also called formal sector.

Benefits to Workers

Workers of the organised sector enjoy the following benefits :

- They enjoy job security.
- They work only for a fixed number of hours. If they work more, they have to be paid overtime by the employer.
- They also get social security benefits from their employers like provident fund, gratuity, pension, etc.
- They also get paid leaves, medical benefits under the laws clean drinking water and safe working environment.

Unorganised Sector

Unorganised sector is not registered by the government. There are rules and regulations but these are not followed.

It includes all unlicensed, self-employed or unregistered economic activities, such as owner-manned general stores, handicrafts and handloom workers, rural traders and farmers. About 90% of India's workforce is a part of this sector.

Main Features of Unorganised Sector

(Or Disadvantages to Workers)

(i) Jobs are low paid and also often not regular.

(ii) There is no job security.

(iii) There is no provision for overtime, paid leave, holidays and sick leave.

(iv) Hours of work are also not fixed.

We can now summarise the difference between the organised and unorganised sectors as in Table 2.3.

Table 2.3 : Difference between Organised and Unorganised Sectors

S. No.	Basis	Organised Sector	Unorganised Sector
1.	Registration	The enterprises of this sector are registered by the government.	This sector is not registered by the government.
2.	Scope	It includes those enterprises or places of work where terms and conditions of employment are fixed.	This sector covers small and unincorporated enterprises, self employed people and millions of farmers.
3.	Rules and Regulations	This sector is governed by government rules and regulations.	This sector is not governed by government rules and regulations.
4.	Alternative name	This sector is also known as formal sector.	This is also called informal sector.

How to protect workers in the unorganised sector?

The job opportunities in organised sector are very limited. As a result, a large number of people are forced to enter the unorganised sector to earn their livelihoods. As we have studied in the preceding section, the working conditions in the unorganised sector are very poor. The workers are often exploited here. Hence, the need of hour is to protect the interest of the workers in the unorganised sector (Refer Table 2.4).

Table 2.4 : Comparison of Unorganised Sector in Rural and Urban Areas

Rural Areas	Urban Areas
• Landless agricultural labourers	• Workers in small industries
• Small and marginal farmers	• Casual workers in construction, trade and transport
• Share croppers	• Street vendors
• Artisans (e.g., weavers, blacksmiths carpenters, goldsmiths)	• Headload workers, Garment makers, Rag pickers

Protection and support to the unorganised sector workers is thus necessary for both economic and social development. Workers in the unorganised sector can be protected in the following ways :

(i) Creating ample job opportunities in the non-farm sector.

(ii) Organising public work programmes like construction of roads, school buildings, digging of irrigation canals to provide employment to the rural workers throughout the year.

(iii) Introducing some social security measures by the government for such workers.

Sectors on the basis of ownership

On the basis of ownership of assets, the economic activities can be broadly classified into two sectors : private sector and public sector.

Private Sector

Private sector refers to all those occupations and economic activities which are privately owned and controlled. It includes all those institutions which are engaged in the production and distribution of goods or services and are in private hands. This sector is mainly guided by the motive of profit.

At present, a major part of our economic activities are in the private sector. About 80% of country's economic activities are carried out in this sector. Agriculture, retail trade, cottage industries, professionals such as doctors, advocates, chartered accountants, etc., normally come under private sector. Most of the big companies are also in the hands of private sector in India. Tata Iron and Steel Company, Reliance, Bajaj Auto and Infosys are the examples of private sector companies.

Public Sector

Public sector implies all those occupations and economic activities owned and controlled by the government. In other words, the sector of production which is under complete control of government is termed as public sector. Public sector undertakings may be under the control of central government, state governments and joint control of central and state governments. These industries are generally termed as Public Sector Undertaking (PSUs). These PSUs include Railways, Post and Telegraph, Steel Authority of India Limited (SAIL), National Thermal Power Corporation (NTPC), etc.

Role of Public Sector

Now we shall see why India has given importance to public sector in its economy. This can be judged from following facts :

1. **Development of Infrastructure:** Development of infrastructure is an essential requirement for rapid economic development of the country. Without the development of infrastructural facilities (e.g., transport, communication, power, irrigation, education, basic industries, etc.) economic development is not possible. These infrastructural facilities are developed only by the public sector of the country because private sector does not take interest in their development due to lack of resources and less profitability. Thus governments have to undertake such heavy spendings and ensure that these facilities are available for everyone.

2. **Government Support in Some Activities :** There are some activities which require government support and encouragement in public interest.

For example, government has to provide electricity to many units especially, small-scale units at subsidised rate, otherwise they might have to shut down. Similarly, our government protects the interest of both farmers and consumers through public distribution system (PDS).

Under the PDS, the government procures foodgrains from the farmers at the pre-announced prices and make it available to the poorer sections of the society at lower prices. The government bears some of the cost.

3. **Provides Basic Facilities :** There are some activities which are regarded as the **prime responsibility of the government**. Hence government must spend on such activities. For example, providing education, health and sanitation facilities are the duties of the government. Similarly, we know that nearly half of India's children are malnourished. Government should also spend money on the welfare of children and on the aspects of human development, availability of safe drinking water, housing facilities for the poor and food and nutrition. It is also the duty of the government to take care of the poorest and most ignored regions of the country through its increased spendings.

GLOSSARY

Organised sector : It is a sector where the employment terms are fixed and regular, and the employees get assured work.

Unorganised sector : It is a sector where the employment terms are not fixed and regular, as well as the enterprises are not registered with the government.

Private sector : It is the part of a country's economic system that is run by individuals and companies, rather than the government.

Public sector : This Sector is owned and operated by the government and exist to provide a range of governmental services, including infrastructure, public transportation, public education, health care, police and military services.

Public distribution system : It is a government-sponsored chain of shops entrusted with the work of distributing basic food and non-food commodities to the needy sections of the society at very cheap prices.

LET'S RECAPITULATE

- On the basis of terms and conditions of employment, economic activities can be divided into organised and unorganised sectors.
- Organised sector covers those enterprises or places of work where there are rules and regulations of work and people get regular and assured employment.
- Unorganised sector is not registered by the government and rules and regulations are not followed.
- Unorganised workers are often exploited. They are paid low wages. There is no job security for them. And also they have to work under unhygienic conditions.
- Protection and support to the unorganised sector workers is necessary on the issues like wages, safety and health.
- On the basis of ownership of assets, the economic activities can be broadly classified into two sectors i.e., private sector and public sector.
- Private sector refers to all those occupations and economic activities which are privately owned and controlled.
- Public sector is the sector of production which is under complete control of central and state governments.
- India has given importance to the public sector because it

  (i) develops infrastructure (ii) provides support in some activities

  (iii) provides basic facilities

CHECK YOUR UNDERSTANDING

1. What is the percentage of people in the unorganised sector in agriculture?
2. Explain disguised unemployment with the help of an example.
3. Why did government create Mahatma Gandhi National Rural Employment Guarantee Act (MGNREGA) in 2005?
4. Look at the following examples. Which of these are unoraganised sector activities?
   (i) A teacher taking classes in a school
   (ii) A headload worker carrying a bag of cement on his back in a market
   (iii) A farmer irrigating his/her field
   (iv) A doctor in a hospital treating a patient
   (v) A daily-wage labourer working under a contractor
   (vi) A factory worker going to work in a big factory
   (vii) A handloom weaver working in his/her house
5. Differentiate between private sector and public sector using some examples.
6. What is the motive of private sector?
7. Why should the government construct roads and build dams?

EXERCISES

I. A. Multiple choice questions.

1. Identify primary sector activity from the following
   (a) Banking (b) Construction (c) Fishing (d) Manufacturing
2. Identify tertiary sector activity from the following
   (a) Transportation (b) Communication (c) Banking (d) All of these
3. Dairy comes under
   (a) Primary sector (b) Secondary sector (c) Tertiary sector (d) Public sector
4. Which of the following profession belongs to the tertiary sector of economy? [CBSE Sample Question Paper 2019-20]
   (a) Fisherman (b) Farmer (c) Factory worker (d) Teacher
5. Mahatma Gandhi National Rural Employment Guarantee Act 2005 is referred to
   (a) Right to Education (b) Right to Information
   (c) Right to Work (d) Right to Vote
6. Intermediate goods refer to those goods which are used in the production of
   (a) Final goods and services (b) Primary goods
   (c) Manufactured goods (d) Other goods and services as raw-materials
7. Final goods are those goods which are used
   (a) for final consumption (b) for investment
   (c) both (a) and (b) (d) neither (a) nor (b)
8. Which is true about the Indian economy?
   (a) Primary sector is the largest contributor to country's GDP.
   (b) Secondary sector is the largest sector of the economy.
   (c) The importance of primary sector is rising.
   (d) Service sector has emerged as the largest producing sector.

9. On the basis of ownership over assets, an economy is classified into
(a) Private and public sectors
(b) Organised and unorganised sectors
(c) Primary, secondary and tertiary sectors
(d) Rural and urban sectors

10. Disguised unemployment refers to a situation when
(a) people are willing to work but they don't find work.
(b) people do not want to work voluntarily.
(c) more people are employed than are actually required.
(d) people become unemployed during off season.

11. Which one of the following activities does not belong to the primary sector? [CBSE 2011]
(a) Agriculture (b) Dairy (c) Mining (d) Weaving

12. Which of the following is an example of the service sector? [CBSE 2011]
(a) Horticulture (b) Pottery making (c) Dairy farming (d) Storage

13. Which one of the following sectors is the largest employer in India? [CBSE 2011]
(a) Primary (b) Secondary (c) Tertiary (d) IT sector

14. Tertiary sector has become an important part of Indian economy on account of [CBSE 2011]
(a) development of agriculture and industry
(b) rise in levels of income
(c) both (a) and (b)
(d) none of these

15. Workers enjoy job security in [CBSE 2011]
(a) agriculture sector (b) private sector (c) unorganised sector (d) organised sector

16. Which of the following acts would not apply to a company like TISCO? [CBSE 2011]
(a) Minimum Wages Act
(b) National Rural Employment Guarantee Act
(c) Factories Act
(d) Payment of Gratuity Act

17. Disguised unemployment means a situation where people are [CBSE 2011]
(a) unemployed
(b) employed but earning less salary
(c) employed but work less than their potential
(d) unemployed for a short period of time

18. Underemployment is a situation when people [CBSE 2011]
(a) do not want to work
(b) are not paid for their work
(c) are working in a lazy manner
(d) want to do job, but not getting job

19. Identify the feature of the unorganised sector. [CBSE 2011]
(a) Rules and regulations are followed.
(b) Workers enjoy security of employment.
(c) Employment is not secure.
(d) It follows some formal processes and procedure.

20. Which of the following is not applicable for a worker, who works in the organised sector? [CBSE 2011]
(a) He/she gets a regular salary at the end of the month.
(b) He/she is not paid for leave.
(c) He/she gets medical allowance.
(d) He/she got an appointment letter stating the terms and conditions of work when he/she joined this work.

21. Which of the following statement is true in respect of public sector? [CBSE 2011]
(a) Big companies own most of the assets.
(b) Government owns the assets.
(c) A group of people owns most of the assets.
(d) An individual owns most of the assets.

22. Public enterprises are owned by [CBSE 2011]
(a) individual owners.
(b) government.
(c) both government and individual.
(d) none of the above

23. The sectors are classified into public and private sector on the basis of [CBSE 2011]
(a) employment conditions.
(b) the nature of economic activities.
(c) number of worker employed.
(d) ownership of enterprise.

24. The motive of public sector enterprises is [CBSE 2011]
(a) profit making.
(b) entertainment.
(c) social welfare and security.
(d) none of these

25. Railways is an example of [CBSE 2011]
(a) Private sector.
(b) Public sector.
(c) Secondary sector.
(d) none of these

26. For how many days employment assurance has been provided under MGNREGA Act?
(a) 150 days (b) 365 days (c) 200 days (d) 100 days

27. The Government of India has implemented the Right to Work in [CBSE 2011]
(a) 2004 (b) 2005 (c) 2006 (d) 2007

28. Which of the following was the objective of MGNREGA 2005? [CBSE 2011]
(a) To control the unorganised sector in rural areas
(b) To provide 100 days employment in a year by the government
(c) To control the flow of money from private sector to public sector
(d) None of the above

29. The motive of private sector enterprises is
(a) profit making
(b) entertainment
(c) social welfare and security
(d) none of these

30. Arrange the following in the correct sequence. [CBSE Sample Question Paper 2019-20]
(i) Transporting cloth to the workshops
(ii) Sale in shops and showrooms
(iii) Spinning the yarn
(iv) Weaving of the fabric

Mark the correct option :
(a) (i)-(iv)-(iii)-(ii) (b) (iii)-(iv)-(i)-(ii) (c) (iv)-(i)-(ii)-(iii) (d) (iii)-(iv)-(ii)-(i)

B. Match the following terms given in Column A with those in Column

Column A		Column B	
A.	Primary sector activity	1.	Banking
B.	Secondary sector activity	2.	Rules and regulations of work
C.	Tertiary sector activity	3.	Fishing
D.	Organised sector	4.	Weaving of the fabric

C. Which of the following are organised sector activities :

(i) a person working as manager in a bank
(ii) a construction worker working on daily basis
(iii) a cook working as a domestic help
(iv) a peon working in a multinational company
(v) an engineer working in a construction company
(vi) a doctor working in his own clinic
(vii) a teacher working in a government school

Mark the correct option :
(a) (vii)-(ii)-(iii)-(i) (b) (i)-(iv)-(v)-(vii) (c) (v)-(ii)-(vi)-(vii) (d) (vi)-(vii)-(iv)-(iii)

D. Fill in the blanks.

1. Most of the workers in the ______________ sector enjoy job security.
2. About ______________ percent of labourers in India are working in the unorganised sector.
3. Cotton is a ______________ product.
4. Production of a commodity, mostly through the natural process is an activity in ______________sector.

5. The full form of GDP is ______________.

6. There has been a remarkable change in the share of the three sectors in GDP, a similarly shift has not taken place in ______________. [CBSE 2016]

7. Private sector activities are guided by the motive of ______________.

8. ______________ includes those enterprises where terms of employment are regular.

9. A daily wage labourer comes under ______________ sector of the economy.

II. A. Very short answer type questions.

1. Give two examples of primary activities.
2. What is the other name of Primary sector? [CBSE 2015]
3. What do you mean by tertiary sector? [CBSE 2015]
4. Name any two activities which are associated with the tertiary sector. [CBSE 2011]
5. What are secondary activities? Give example.
6. Define the term intermediate goods.
7. What are final goods? Give two examples of tertiary sector activities.
8. Define Gross Domestic Product.
9. Why is the value of intermediate goods not included in country's GDP?
10. State the meaning of under employment. [CBSE 2016]
11. What is another name of disguised unemployment? [CBSE 2016]
12. What is MGNREGA?
13. In which year National Rural Employment Guarantee Act was implemented? [CBSE 2016]

    OR

    Write one objective of National Rural Employment Guarantee Act 2005.
14. What is meant by disguised unemployment (or underemployment)?
15. What are the main sectors into which Indian economy is classified on the basis of ownership?

    OR

    State the basis on which the sectors of economy are classified into public and private? [CBSE 2017]
16. Why are all the family members of a farmer engaged on the farm though they are not required?
17. Give one measure which can help in generating more employment in our agricultural sector.
18. What do you mean by organised sector?
19. Give two examples of public sector companies.
20. Why is the secondary sector called the manufacturing sector?
21. Why is MGNREGA also called the Right to Work? [CBSE 2015]
22. How many days of guaranteed employment are provided under National Rural Employment Guarantee Act 2005? [CBSE 2015]

B. Short answer type questions.

1. What is gross domestic product? Why is the value of intermediate goods not included to calculate GDP? [CBSE 2016]
2. How will you calculate the GDP of a country? [CBSE 2015]

3. Differentiate between intermediate goods and final goods using examples.
4. Why is it necessary to give protection to unorganised sector workers?
5. Explain how primary sector and secondary sector are interdependent upon each sector.
6. Classify economic activities on the basis of ownership. Mention one feature of each. [CBSE 2016]
7. Mention the features of MGNREGA?
8. How does the government support the private sector?
9. Which occupation belongs to primary sector? Mention any one. [CBSE 2016]
10. Compare the employment conditions prevailing in the organised and the unorganised sectors. [CBSE 2015]
11. Elaborate the employment conditions of people working in the unorganised sector? [CBSE 2015]
12. There has been a big change in the three sectors of economic activities, but a similar shift has not taken place in the share of employment. Explain the above statement on the basis of facts. [CBSE 2012, 2015]
13. Explain the objective of implementing the MGNREGA 2005.

    OR

    Describe the objective of implementing MGNREGA 2005. [CBSE 2011, 2016]

    OR

    What was the main objective of MGNREGA? [CBSE 2016]

    OR

    How many days work (employment) guarantee provided by Government under MGNREGA-2005? [CBSE 2015]

    OR

    Why do you think MGNREGA, 2005 is referred to as Right To Work? [CBSE 2015]
14. Differentiate between open unemployment and disguised unemployment.
15. Classify the industries on the basis of employment. [CBSE 2011]
16. Is it necessary to have the public sector? Substantiate your answer by examining the role of the Government. [CBSE 2015]
17. *You are seeking employment.* In which of the sectors–organised or unorganised would you like to work? Justify your answer. [CBSE 2015]
18. Why do people prefer to work in an organised sector? Explain. [CBSE 2015]

C. Long answer type questions.

1. Explain the difference between primary, secondary and tertiary sectors using examples.
2. Differentiate between public sector and private sector citing examples.
3. "The tertiary sector has emerged as the largest producing sector in India". Give reasons.
4. Define organised sector. What are the benefits to labourers working in this sector?
5. Describe in brief the role of public sector in economic development.

    OR

    Explain how public sector contributes to the economic development of a nation.
6. How would income and employment increase if farmers were provided with irrigation facilities?
7. Describe the changes that have taken place in the share of different sectors in India's GDP.

8. Suggest measures to remove disguised unemployment in the agricultural sector.

9. How can we generate more employment in Indian economy? Suggest some measures.

10. What is disguised unemployment? Where does it exist in India?

11. Compare the conditions of employment of organised with that of unorganised sector.

12. "The declining share of primary sector in the Gross Domestic Product (GDP) is a matter of serious concern in India." Support the statement.

13. Differentiate between the public and private sectors in an economy with examples. [CBSE 2015]

OR

Differentiate between the public sector and private sector by giving examples. [CBSE 2015]

OR

Distinguish between public and private sector. [CBSE 2012, 2016]

14. Why is the tertiary sector becoming the most important sector in India?

OR

How does tertiary sector help in the development of primary and secondary sectors? Explain with examples. [CBSE 2008]

OR

Give four reasons for the rising importance of tertiary sector in India. [CBSE 2010]

OR

Why is tertiary sector growing so rapidly in India? Explain it with four reasons? [CBSE 2011]

OR

Explain why service sector is gaining in importance in the global economy. [CBSE 2016]

15. Describe the historical changes that have taken place in sectors of the economy in the developed countries. [CBSE 2012]

16. Explain how a shift has taken place between sectors in developed countries. [CBSE 2011]

ANSWERS

MCQS

1. (c)	2. (d)	3. (a)	4. (d)	5. (c)	6. (d)	7. (c)	8. (d)
9. (a)	10. (c)	11. (d)	12. (d)	13. (a)	14. (a)	15. (d)	16. (b)
17. (c)	18. (d)	19. (c)	20. (b)	21. (b)	22. (b)	23. (d)	24. (c)
25. (b)	26. (d)	27. (b)	28. (b)	29. (a)	30. (b)		

Fill in the blanks

1. Organised	2. 90	3. Natural/primary
4. Primary	5. Gross domestic product	6. Employment
7. Profit	8. Organised	9. Unorganised

3

Money and Credit

OUTLINE OF THE CHAPTER

At the end of the chapter students will come to know about :

- Meaning of Barter Exchange
- Bank Money (Deposits with Banks)
- Formal and Informal Credit

3.1 Meaning of Barter Exchange

Prior to the invention of money, goods and services were exchanged directly for goods and services. This type of system of exchange was known as the '**barter system**' of exchage. *Barter means direct exchange of goods and services.* In other words, barter refers to exchange of goods without the use of money. For example, wheat may be exchanged for cloth, house for horses, etc., or a teacher may be paid wheat or rice as a payment for his/her services. The economy based upon this barter system of exchange is known as 'barter economy' or 'C-C economy' where C stands for commodity.

Difficulty of Barter Exchange

In the barter system, it is necessary for a person, who wishes to trade his goods or services, to find some other person who is not only willing to buy his good or service, but also possesses that good which the former wants. This is known as **double coincidence of wants**. For example, suppose a person possesses rice and wants to exchange it for sugar. In the barter system he has to find out a person who not only has sugar but also wants to take rice in return. But such a double coincidence is a rare possibility. The person would most likely have to undertake some immediate transactions of rice for wheat, wheat for cloth, cloth for wood and finally wood for the desired sugar or he would have to accept something less useful than the sugar.

Example :

This problem of double coincidence of wants can further be illustrated by citing an example.

Lt. Camerein once needed a boat while travelling through Africa. He went to a person who had a boat, but he wanted to exchange boat only for ivory. Then he went to a person who had ivory. But the person who had ivory wanted cloth in exchange for it. Then again Camerein had to search out a person who had cloth. The person who had cloth wanted wire for cloth. Luckily, Camerein had wire with him. So, he first exchanged wire for cloth, then cloth for ivory and finally ivory for the boat he needed. Thus, he had to face a great difficulty to obtain boat to cross the river in Africa. Had he been money with him, he could have avoided this difficulty.

Double Coincidence of Wants

- In a barter system, where goods are directly exchanged without the use of money, double coincidence of wants is very essential.
- When two persons agree to sell and buy each others commodities, this is known as double coincidence of wants.

Due to lack of double coincidence of wants barter exchange involves several intermediate transactions for meeting one particular want.

Medium of Exchange

Money as a medium of exchange means that it is used in buying goods and services.

- It is generally accepted by the people. Therefore, all exchanges of goods and services in an economy take place in terms of money.
- Money itself does not satisfy people's wants, but it has power to buy goods and services that we need.
- Nobody has any objection either in accepting money by giving their own commodities or in giving money for other commodities. Thus, through this medium of money any commodity can be purchased or sold. Thus, money acts as a medium of exchange.
- Money as medium of exchange, separates the acts of sale and purchase of goods and services. If a person wants to buy goods, he can do so with money. And, if wants to sell goods, he can sell these for money.

Measure of Value

Measure of value is the other function of money. Money serves as a measure of value in terms of unit of account. Unit of account means that the value of each good or service is measured in the monetary unit. Measurement of value was the main difficulty of the barter system. Introduction of money has removed this difficulty. When we express the value of a commodity in terms of money, it is known as **price**. Today we express the value of different goods and services in terms of money in every economy. For example, the price of sugar as ₹40 per kg, price of milk as ₹50 per litre, the price of pen as ₹20, monthly salary of a domestic help as ₹6,000 per month, etc.

Modern Forms of Money

Before the introduction of coins, a variety of objects were used as money. For example, in the very early ages in India, we used grains, cattle, leather, metals, etc. as money. Thereafter, we started the use of metallic coins – gold, silver and copper coins and it continued till the last century.

In the modern times we normally use two forms of money :

1. Currency and Paper Notes
2. Bank Money (Deposits with Banks).

Fig. 3.1 : Items such as knife, cow, wheat and shoes were once used as money.

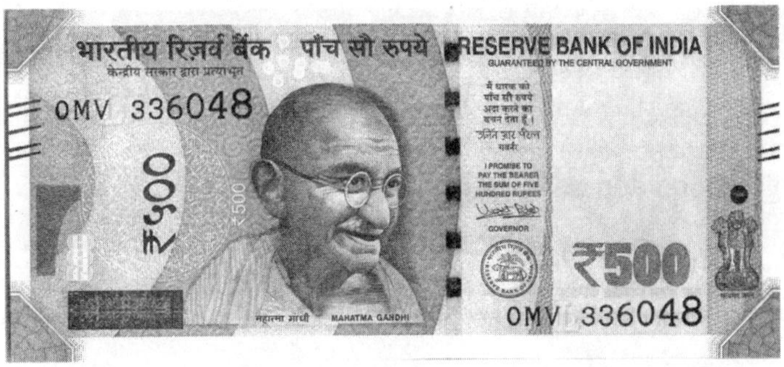

Fig. 3.2 : Today currency (paper notes+coins) and chequable deposits constitute money.

- Currency is an important form of modern money. Each country has its own currency. For example, Rupee in India, Dollar in USA, Pound in United Kingdom and so on.
- Currency can be anything which is authorised by the government of the country. It has to be accepted for transactions.
- Currency includes coins and paper notes. Coins are made of some metals, hence they are called metallic coins. The use of metallic coins presented certain difficulties like transaction, storage, etc. This marked the development of paper notes (or currency notes).
- In every country, the issue of currency is either in the hands of central government or in the hands of central bank. In India, the issue of currency notes is the monopoy of the Reserve Bank of India (RBI).
- In India, the accepted currency is Rupee (₹). This is official medium of payments. No one can refuse to accept it by the government.

Currency = Paper Notes + Coins

GLOSSARY

Barter system : It is a system of exchange where participants in a transaction directly exchange goods or services for other goods or services without using a medium of exchange.

Coincidence of wants: It is an economic phenomenon where two parties each hold an item the other wants, so they exchange these items directly without any monetary medium.

Money : Money is any good that is widely used and accepted in transactions involving the transfer of goods and services from one person to another.

Medium of exchange : It is an intermediary instrument or system used to facilitate the sale, purchase or trade of goods between parties.

Measure of value : It is the function of money that enables the values of different goods and services to be compared, also referred to as a unit of value.

Currency : It is money, in the form of paper or coins, usually issued by a government and generally accepted at its face value as a method of payment.

LET'S RECAPITULATE

- Prior to the invention of money, goods and services were exchanged directly for goods and services and the system was known as Barter System of exchange.
- The economy based upon this barter system is known as 'barter economy' or 'C-C economy' where C stands for commodity.
- In a barter system, where goods are directly exchanged without the use of money, double coincidence of wants is an essential feature.
- Money as a medium of exchange separates the acts of sale and purchase of goods and services.
- Money serves as a measure of value in terms of Unit of Account, i.e., the value of each good or service is measured in the monetary unit.
- In the very early ages in India, we used grains, cattle, leather, metals etc. as money.
- Thereafter, we started the use of metallic coins - gold, silver and copper coins and it continued till the last century.
- Modern forms of money include currency, paper notes and bank money.
- The issue of currency is either in the hands of the central government or in the hands of central bank.
- In India, the accepted currency is Rupee, an official medium of payments and nobody can refuse to accept it.

CHECK YOUR UNDERSTANDING

1. Give the meaning of barter exchange.
2. What is meant by the double coincidence of wants?
3. How does the use of money make it easier to exchange goods and services?
4. Why is money accepted as a 'medium of exchange'?
5. What do you mean by currency and paper notes?

3.2 Bank Money (Deposits with Banks)

The other form in which people keep money is deposits with banks. At a point of time, people do not need all currency they hold, rather only some currency is needed to meet day-to-day cash requirements. The rest (i.e., surplus currency) is deposited in banks. To keep money in terms of deposits in banks is advantageous to them in the following ways :

(i) People's money is safe.

(ii) Banks pay an amount of interest on deposits.

(iii) People can also withdraw the money as and when they require.

There are different types of accounts which are opened by banks. They are different in terms of interest payable and term of deposits. The deposit where money can be withdrawn any time is called demand deposit.

Bank money refers to bank deposits by people with banks which they can withdraw at any time they like. The deposits in the bank accounts that can be withdrawn on demand, are called **demand deposits**.

The banks offer another right to the depositor. He is allowed to make a payment through cheque instead of cash. For payment through cheque, the payer who has an account with the bank writes a cheque for a specific amount. *A cheque is a paper instructing the bank to pay a specific amount from the person's account to the person in whose name the cheque has been made.* Demand deposit, therefore, is an alternative cash transaction (Fig. 3.3). In short,

Money = Currency + Demand deposits

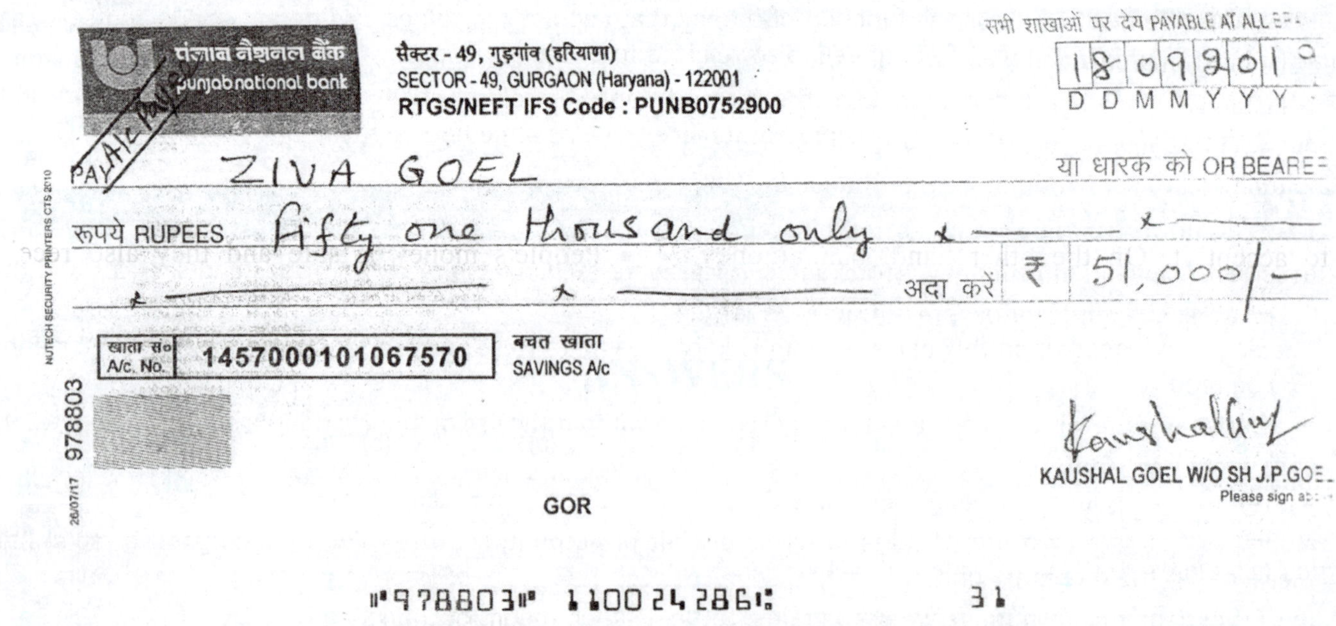
पंजाब नैशनल बैंक punjab national bank
सैक्टर - 49, गुड़गांव (हरियाणा)
SECTOR - 49, GURGAON (Haryana) - 122001
RTGS/NEFT IFS Code : PUNB0752900
A/c Payee
सभी शाखाओं पर देय PAYABLE AT ALL BRA...
18092010
D D M M Y Y Y Y
PAY ZIVA GOEL या धारक को OR BEARER
रुपये RUPEES Fifty one thousand only
अदा करें ₹ 51,000/-
खाता सं. A/c. No. 1457000101067570 बचत खाता SAVINGS A/c
KAUSHAL GOEL W/O SH J.P.GOEL
Please sign above
GOR
NUTECH SECURITY PRINTERS CTS 2010
26/07/17 978803
⑈978803⑈ 110024286⑆ 31

Fig. 3.3 : Demand Deposit – Cheque

It is important to note that the cheque itself is not money. It is the demand deposits against which cheque is written is money. Cheque performs the same function as money, i.e., payments for purchases as medium of exchange. Therefore, demand deposits are also treated as an important form of money.

Advantages of Cheque Payments

(i) It is a convenient mode of payment, as the payer need not go to the bank for cash withdrawal to make payment.

(ii) No cash is needed to make payment. Money is simply transferred from one bank account to another bank account.

(iii) Cheque can be written to exact amount.

(iv) Cheque can be produced as an evidence in the event of any dispute.

Payment through cheque

Let us now understand how payments are made through cheques. Suppose a housewife, Sneh Lata makes some grocery purchases from a provision store. She has to make payment of ₹6,500 for the items purchased. She (having an account with the State Bank of India) simply writes a cheque for ₹6,500 in the name of Ramlal, the owner of the store. Ramlal will then deposit this cheque in his own account with Punjab National Bank. Then Punjab National Bank collects the money from Sneh Lata's bank account with the State Bank of India and deposits in Ramlal's account. In this way, the transaction is complete without the payment of cash.

Currency versus bank money

- Currency and bank money (i.e., demand deposits with banks) are the two forms of money.
- Currency is legal money. Nobody can refuse to accept it. On the other hand, bank money is optional. One is not bound to accept it. The acceptance of cheque is totally optional. However, some legal provisions exist to ensure that people do not cheat others. There is a provision for punishments to defaulters.

Loan activities of banks

Banks perform two important functions : acceptance of deposits and advancing of loans. Thus, on the one hand, banks accept deposits from the public and, on the other hand, they give loans to the needy. Thus, banks act as intermediaries between the depositors and borrowers. We know that banks give interest to the depositors and charge interest from the borrowers. The lending rate is always higher than the deposit rates. The difference between what is charged from borrowers and what is paid to depositors is the main source of income of the banks.

Banks know from their experience that all the depositors do not demand all the money at the same time. So they keep only a small proportion of their deposits as cash reserves with themselves. For example, banks in India these days hold about 15% of their deposits as cash. This is kept as provision to pay the depositors who might come to withdraw money from the bank on any given day. Since, on any particular day, only some of its money depositors come to withdraw money, the bank is able to manage with this money. Hence, keeping a small portion of total deposits as cash reserve, the major portion can be given as loans by the banks. Loans always remain in great demand for various economic activities, say to buy a house, to buy a car, to start or expand a business and so on.

Significance of Bank Deposits

- Deposits with banks are benefical both for individuals as well as for the nation.
- People's money is safe and they also receive interest on their deposits. Moreover, they can also withdraw their money in times of need.
- Banks channelise their deposits for investment in development projects.
- Banks give loans to the needy people like farmers, businessmen etc.

GLOSSARY

Bank : A bank is a financial institution and a financial intermediary that accepts deposits and channels those deposits into lending activities.

Demand deposits : Demand deposit funds are deposited in a bank account at a low or a zero interest rate, which allows depositors to directly withdraw their money and issue bank cheques up to the limit of their account balance at any time.

Cheque : A cheque is a document that orders a bank to pay a specific amount of money from a person's account to the person in whose name the cheque has been issued.

Currency : It is money, in the form of paper or coins, usually issued by a central government and generally accepted at its face value as a method of payment.

Loan : A loan is when you receive money from a friend, bank or financial institution in exchange for future repayment of the principal, plus interest.

LET'S RECAPITULATE

- People hold money in the form of deposits with banks as only some currency is needed to meet day-to-day cash requirements.
- There are different types of accounts opened by banks in terms of interest payable and the terms of deposits.
- Bank money refers to the bank deposits by people with banks which they can withdraw at any time they like.
- Deposits in bank account that can be withdrawn on demand are called demand deposits.
- A cheque is a paper instructing the bank to pay a specific amount from the person's account to the person in whose name the cheque has been made or issued.
- Banks, on one hand, accept deposits and give interest to the depositors, and on the other hand, banks give loans to the borrowers and charge interest from borrowers.
- The difference between what is charged from borrowers and what is paid to the depositors is the main source of income of the banks.
- Deposits with banks are beneficial for individuals as well as for the nation.

CHECK YOUR UNDERSTANDING

1. Define the term 'Demand deposits'.
2. Why are demand deposits considered as money?
3. What would happen if all the depositors ask their money from bank at the same time?
4. Why is money accepted as a medium of exchange?
5. State the advantages of cheque payments.

3.3 FORMAL AND INFORMAL CREDIT

Meaning of Credit

A large number of transactions in our day-to-day activities involves credit in some form or the other. *Credit (loan) refers to an agreement in which the lender supplies the borrower with money, goods or services in return for the promise of future payment.*

Importance of Credit

Credit is important due to following reasons :

(i) Credit helps the people to purchase houses.

(ii) Credit helps the businessman to expand their business. It helps them to complete production on time and thereby increase their earnings.

(iii) The difference between the lending rate and borrowing rate is the souce of income for the banks.

(iv) In rural areas, the main demand for credit comes for crop production which involves considerable cost of seeds, fertilisers, pesticides, water, electricals, repair of equipment, etc. Farmers usually take crop loans at the beginning of the season and repay the loan after harvesting the crop.

Thus, credit encompasses investment in the country which creates employment opportunities. It stimulates the economic activities in the country.

Different Credit Situations

When a person takes credit, how does it affect him? This we can understand with the help of some examples given below.

Example 1. Credit Taken by Sohan Lal, a Businessman. Sohan Lal has received a large order to supply school uniforms within 2 months time. To complete this on time, he has to increase production of school uniform. For this he has to purchse raw materials. He has also to hire more labourers. He takes loans from two sources. *First*, he asks the cloth supplier to supply cloth now and promises to pay him later after 2 months. *Second*, he takes loan of some cash in the form of advance money from the larger trader.

After 2 months Sohan Lal delivers the supply of school uniform on time. In this transaction, he makes a good profit and repays the loan he has taken.

Example 2. Credit Taken by a Small Farmer. Now we look into the different credit situations in which Savita, a small farmer, owing one hectare of land takes loan from the village moneylender. She has takes loan to meet the expenses of cultivation. She hopes that she would repay the loan after the harvest. Unfortunately the crop fails, she could not earn to repay the loan and the loan grows into a large amount, because moneylender charges a very high interest rate. Next year also, Savita takes a fresh loan hoping to manage the repayment of loans of both the years from the earnings of this crop. She has a normal crop this year. But the earnings from the crop are not enough to repay the previous loan. She has to sell a part of the land to repay the old debt.

Therefore we conclude that : Whether credit would be useful or not depend on the risks in the situation.

Example 3. A Home Loan. Suppose Sunita a doctor in a hospital, takes a loan of ₹40 lakh from the State Bank of India to purchase a flat in Gurugram. The rate of interest on home loan is 9% per annum and the loan is to be repaid in 20 years through monthly installments. The payment of installment will be deducted directly from the salary of Sunita by the hospital. Sunita is asked to submit the following documents before the sanctioning of the loan amount.

(a) Employment record

(b) Annual salary

(c) Collateral papers, i.e., property papers.

Terms of Credit

When a borrower takes loan (or credit) from a creditor, he has to pay the lender a specified rate of interest along with the repayment of principal. Loans may be granted on security or without security. Mostly lenders demand collateral (security) against loans.

Collateral is an asset that the borrower owns (e.g., land, building, vehicle, livestock, stock of goods, bank deposits) and uses it as a guarantee to a lender. The collateral remains under the charge of the lender until the loan is repaid. If the borrower fails to repay the loan, the lender has the right to get the money by selling the asset of the borrower.

The collateral, rate of interest, documentation requirement, mode of payment, penalties together constitute **terms of credit**. The terms of agreement vary substantially from borrower to borrower.

Documentation requirements include date of birth proof, ration card, identity card, pay slip, photograph, paper of land, etc.

Terms of Credit
OR
Requirements to get a bank loan

- Interest rate
- Collateral (security)
- Documentation requirement
- Mode of payment

FORMAL SECTOR CREDIT IN INDIA

The various types of loans can be grouped into two categories :

1. Formal sector loans and
2. Informal sector loans.

- Formal sector loans include loans from banks and cooperatives. The informal sector lenders include moneylender, traders, employees, relatives and friends, etc.

The share of various sources of credit to rural households in India is shown in Fig. 3.4, below.

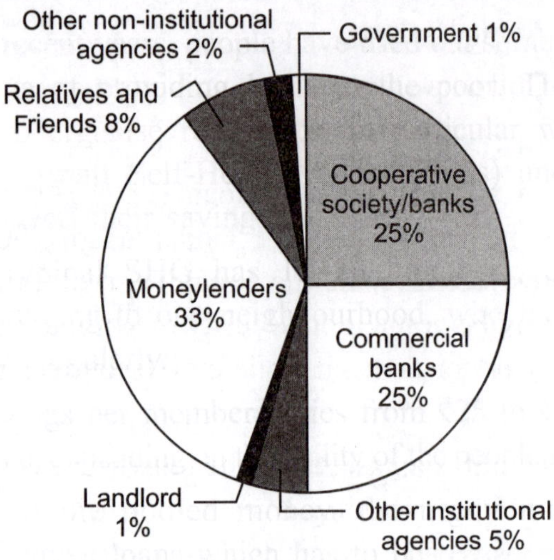

Fig. 3.4 : Sources of credit per ₹1000 of rural households in India (2012)

(i) Cooperatives and Commercial Banks. In the total credit to rural households, the share of formal sector is 50% [cooperatives (25%) + commercial banks (25%)]. And the rest 50% of the total credit comes from informal sources. This shows that even today informal lending occupies an important place in the total rural credit.

(ii) Moneylenders. Among the informal sources, the share of moneylenders (33%) is the largest. Though moneylenders charge very high rate of interest, they provide loans without collateral. That is why, most of the poor who have no collateral to offer, approach them for their loan requirements. The share of relatives and friends is 8%.

(iii) Government and Other Formal Sources. The central government and state governments also provide credit to farmers through various schemes. The share of government and other formal sources is just 6%.

- The RBI supervises the activities of the banks. It is mandatory for the banks to maintain a minimum cash reserves out of the deposits they receive. The RBI monitors the interest rates and the types of loans given by them.

WHY IS SUPERVISION FOR FORMAL SOURCES OF CREDIT NECESSARY?

The supervision of formal sources of credit is necessary

1. to ensure that credit reaches all segments of the society.
2. to ensure that banks maintain the required cash reserves with themselves.
3. to monitor interest rates and types of loans given by banks.

- On the other hand, there is no organisation which supervises the credit activities of lenders in the informal sector. They can lend at whatever interest rate they decide. They charge a high interest rate on loans given. It means a larger part of the earnings of the borrower goes to the repayment of loan. In certain cases, the amount to be repaid is greater than the income of the borrower. This could lead to debt trap.

The difference between formal sector credit and informal sector credit can be summarised in Table 3.1 below.

Table 3.1 : Formal and Informal Sector Credit

S. No.	Basis	Formal Sector Credit	Informal Sector Credit
1.	**Control**	The Reserve Bank of India supervises the loan activities of formal sources.	There is no organisation to control informal sources of credit.
2.	**Rate of interest**	Interest on loans is low.	Interest on loan is very high.
3.	**Sources of credit**	It is provided by banks and cooperatives.	It is provided by moneylenders, traders, employers, relatives and friends.
4.	**Beneficiaries**	Most of the rich people get formal sector credit. About 90% rich people get loans from this source.	Most of the poor people get loan from this source.

Formal and Informal Credit : Who Gets What?

Like rural borrowers, urban borrowers also take loans from formal and informal sources. The importance of formal and informal sources is not the same for different categories of borrowers. To understand this, urban people are divided into four groups. These are : (i) poor households, (ii) households with a few assets, (iii) well-off households and (iv) rich households.

The share of formal and informal sources of credit among these categories of urban borrowers is given in Table 3.2 and Fig. 3.5.

Table 3.2 : Percentage Share of Formal and Informal Sources of Credit

	Categories of Urban Households			
Sources of Credit	**Poor Households**	**Households with a few Assets**	**Well-off Households**	**Rich Households**
Formal Sector	15%	47%	72%	90%
Informal Sector	85%	53%	28%	10%

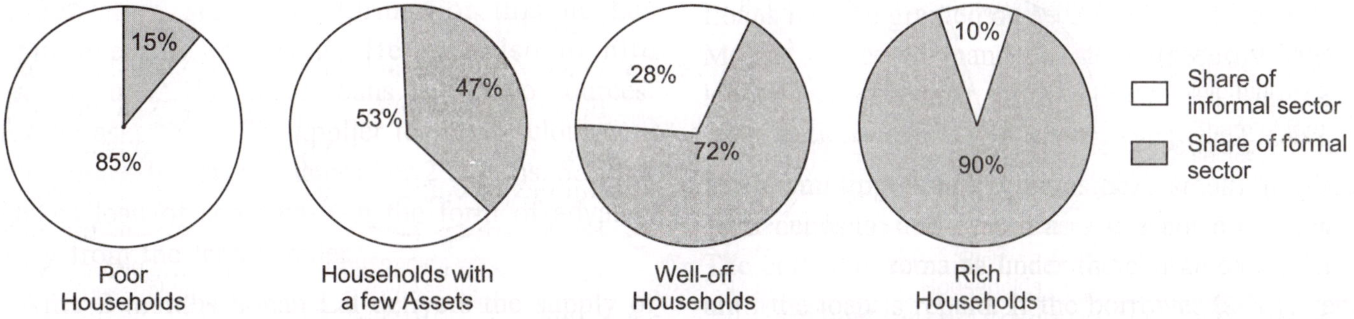

Fig. 3.5 : Percentage Share of Formal and Informal Sources of Credit

From the Table 3.2 and Fig. 3.5 we see that

(a) 85% of the loans taken by the poor households in the urban areas are from informal sources, while they get only 15% loans from the formal sector.

(b) Rich households receive 90% loans from formal sector and only 10% from informal sector. This implies that rich households are availing cheaper credit from formal lenders whereas poor households have to pay much higher interest rates.

Suggestions

On the basis of above discussion, following measures become necessary :

(i) Banks and cooperatives need to increase their lending particularly in the rural areas. This would help in reducing the dependence on informal sources and in increasing their earnings.

(ii) In rural areas, the demand for credit mainly comes from the farmers for crop production. Banks and cooperative provide cheap and affordable credit. This would enhance income of the rural households.

(iii) There is a need to increase the share of formal sector lending in the total credit of the country. Besides this, it should also be taken care of that everyone in the country receives formal sector loans. At present, it is the rich households who receive formal credit whereas the poor has to depend on the informal sources. It is important that the formal credit is distributed more equally so that the poor can get benefit from the cheaper credit.

Why do poor households largely depend on informal sources of credit?

Poor households largely depend on informal sources of credit because of the following reasons :

(i) Bank facilities are not everywhere in rural India.

(ii) There are a large number of formalities for availing bank credit.

(iii) Banks generally insist on collateral security which rural poor are unable to offer.

(iv) Moneylenders know the borrowers personally and are ever ready to advance loans to the rural poor.

Self-Help Groups for the poor

In the previous section we have seen that poor households are still dependent on informal sources of credit due to several difficulties in getting formal credit.

- In recent years, people have tried out some newer ways of providing loans to the poor. The idea is to organise rural poor, in particular women, into small Self-Help Groups (SHGs) and pool (collect) their savings.
- A typical SHG has 15–20 members, usually belonging to one neighbourhood, who meet and save regularly.
- Savings per member varies from ₹25 to ₹100 or more, depending on the ability of the people to save.
- From the pooled money, the needy members are given loans which has to be repaid in small installments over a period of time.
- Small loans are provided to the members for releasing mortgaged land, for meeting working capital needs (e.g., buying seeds, fertilisers, raw materials like bamboo and cloth), for housing materials, for acquiring assets like sewing machine, handlooms, cattle, etc.
- The group charges interest on loans which is much less than what the moneylender charges.
- Loan is sanctioned in the name of the group and is meant to create self-employment opportunities for the members.
- Most of the important decisions regarding the savings and loan activities are taken by the group members.
- Once the SHG achieves maturity in its financial behaviour (which generally takes a period of one year of its formation) it is considered for linking to bank.
- Banks are encouraged to give loans to the SHGs in certain multiples of their accumulated savings.
- Loans are provided to SHGs without any collateral.
- Banks are willing to lend to the poor women when organised in SHGs, to make them self-reliant.

Grameen Bank of Bangladesh

Grameen Bank of Bangladesh is one of the biggest success stories in reaching the poor to meet their credit needs at reasonable rates. The bank was started in 1970s as a small project. In 2018 it had over 9 million members in about 81,600 villages spread across Bangladesh. Most of the borrowers are women belonging to poorest sections of the society.

GLOSSARY

Credit : It is generally defined as a contractual agreement in which a borrower receives something of value now and agrees to repay the lender at a later date - generally with interest.

Collateral : It is an asset that a lender accepts as security for extending a loan and if the borrower defaults on her loan payments, the lender may seize the collateral and sells it to recoup some or all of his losses.

Formal sector credit : Banks and cooperative societies constitute the formal sources of credit and the credit activities are supervised by the Reserve Bank of India.

Informal sector credit : Landlords, moneylenders, traders, relatives, friends and other sources of credit constitute the informal sector of credit.

Self-Help Group : A self-Help Group is a financial intermediary committee usually composed of 15-20 local women or men.

LET'S RECAPITULATE

- Credit refers to an agreement in which the lender supplies the borrower with money, goods or services in return for the promise of future payment.
- Credit encompasses investment in the country which creates employment opportunities and stimulates economic activities in the country.

- Collateral is an asset that the borrower owns and uses it as a guarantee to a lender.
- The collateral, rate of interest, documentation requirement, mode of payment and penalties together constitute the terms of credit.
- The various types of loans can be grouped into two categories, i.e., formal sector loans and informal sector loans.
- Formal sector loans include loans from banks and cooperatives, whereas the informal sector lenders include moneylenders, traders, employees, relatives, friends, etc.
- The supervision of formal sources of credit is necessary to monitor interest rates, types of loans given by banks.
- In India, banks and cooperatives need to increase their lending particularly in the rural areas.
- In India, credit arrangements are not fair to all sections of society. Rich households get a major share in total formal credit compared to the poor households. Most of the lending institutions are located in urban areas.
- In recent years, men and women in rural areas organise into small Self-Help Groups (SHGs) to pool their savings and arrange for timely loans for a variety of purposes at a reasonable rate of interest.

CHECK YOUR UNDERSTANDING

1. What do you understand by collateral?
2. State the meaning of 'terms of credit'.
3. What are the informal sources of credit?
4. Why should credit be available to all at reasonable rate of interest?
5. Why is the share of formal credit higher for the rich households compared to the poor households?
6. Why do poor people still take loan from informal sources of credit?

EXERCISES

I. A. Multiple choice questions.

1. Name the system in which the double coincidence of wants is an essential feature. [CBSE 2011]
   (a) Barter system (b) Money economy (c) Global economy (d) None of these
2. Which out of the following is not included in the money?
   (a) ATM card (b) Paper notes (c) Coins (d) Demand deposits
3. Which one of the following is the important characteristic of modern form of currency? [CBSE 2011]
   (a) It is made from precious metal.
   (b) It is made from thing of everyday use.
   (c) It is authorised by commerical banks.
   (d) It is authorised by the government of the country.
4. Which of the following institutions is authorised to issue currency in India? [CBSE 2011]
   (a) Reserve Bank of India (b) Bank of India (c) Parliament of India (d) State Bank of India
5. Which one of the following is not a modern form of money? [CBSE 2011]
   (a) Demand deposits (b) Paper currency (c) Coins (d) Precious metals
6. Which one of the following is not an example of informal sector loans for poor rural household in India? [CBSE 2011]
   (a) Commercial banks (b) Moneylenders (c) Traders (d) Landlords
7. Identify the formal source of credit. [CBSE 2011]
   (a) Banks (b) Moneylenders (c) Traders (d) Landlords

8. Which of the following is a formal source of credit? [CBSE 2017]
(a) Friends (b) Relatives (c) Moneylenders (d) Cooperative society

9. Which one of the following is the main source of credit for rich urban households? [CBSE 2013]
(a) Moneylenders (b) Businessmen (c) Banks (d) Self-Help Groups

10. Which of the following is the main informal source of credit for rural households in India? [CBSE 2013]
(a) Friends (b) Relatives (c) Landlords (d) Moneylenders

11. ______________ is an informal source of credit.
(a) Moneylender (b) State Bank of India
(c) Punjab National Bank (d) Cooperative Bank

12. ______________ is the main source of credit for rural households.
(a) Moneylenders (b) Landlords (c) Traders (d) Banks

13. Which one of the following is the appropriate meaning of collateral? [CBSE 2011]
(a) It is the total sum of money borrowed from banks.
(b) It is the amount of money borrowed from friends.
(c) It is an asset of the borrower used as guarantee to a lender.
(d) It is the total amount of money invested in a business.

14. Which one of the following is a major reason that prevents the poor from getting loans from the banks?
(a) Lack of capital [CBSE 2011]
(b) Not affordable due to high rate of interest
(c) Absence of collateral security
(d) Absence of mediators

15. In a SHG most of the decisions regarding loan activities are taken by [CBSE 2011]
(a) Banks (b) Members
(c) Non-government organisation (d) Cooperatives

B. Find the incorrect option. [CBSE Sample Question Paper 2019-20]
(a) Demand deposits share the essential features of money.
(b) With demand deposit, payments can be made without cash.
(c) Demand deposits are safe way of money transformation.
(d) Demand deposit facility is like cheque.

C. Rita has taken a loan of ₹7 lakhs from the bank to purchase a car. The annual interest rate on the loan is 14.5% and the loan is to be repaid in 3 years in monthly installments. The bank retained the papers of the new car as collateral, which will be returned to Rita only when she repays the entire loan with interest.
[CBSE Sample Question Paper 2019-20]

Analyse the loan information given above, considering one of the following correct option.
(a) Mode of repayment (b) Terms of credit
(c) Interest on loan (d) Deposit criteria

D. Arrange the following in the correct sequence.
(i) repayment of loan (ii) growing crop
(iii) sale of farm produce (iv) borrowing by farmer from moneylender

Mark the correct option.
(a) (iv)-(ii)-(iii)-(i) (b) (i)-(iii)-(ii)-(iv)
(c) (iii)-(iv)-(ii)-(i) (d) (ii)-(iii)-(i)-(iv)

E. Match the following items given in Column A with those in Column B correctly.

1.

Column A		Column B	
A.	Exchange of shoes for wheat	(i)	Medium of exchange
B.	Problem of barter exchange	(ii)	Coincidence of wants
C.	Function of money	(iii)	Barter exchange
D.	Two persons agree to sell and buy each other commodity	(iv)	Problem of double coincidence of wants

Mark the correct option.

(a) (ii)-(iv)-(i)-(iii) (b) (iv)-(iii)-(ii)-(i) (c) (iii)-(iv)-(i)-(ii) (d) (ii)-(i)-(iv)-(iii)

2.

Column A		Column B	
A.	Currency	(i)	Bank money
B.	Modern forms of money	(ii)	Payment through cheque
C.	Demand deposits	(iii)	Paper notes + Coins
D.	No cash is needed to make payment	(iv)	Currency + Demand deposits

Mark the correct option.

(a) (ii)-(i)-(iv)-(iii) (b) (iii)-(ii)-(iv)-(i) (c) (iv)-(iii)-(i)-(ii) (d) (iii)-(iv)-(i)-(ii)

F. Fill in the blanks.

1. ____________ is the main difficulty faced under barter system.
2. ____________ is legal money.
3. ____________ is optional money.
4. Majority of the credit needs of the ____________ households are met from formal sources of credit.
5. ____________ issues currency-notes on behalf of the central government.
6. Banks charge a higher interest rate on loans than what they offer on ____________.
7. ____________ and ____________ are the two major sources of formal sector credit in India.

II. A. Very short answer type questions.

1. What is the meaning of barter system? [CBSE 2015]
2. What do you understand by the term 'double coincidence of wants'?

   OR

   Recognise the situation when both the parties in a barter economy have to agree to sell and buy each other's commodities. What is it called? [CBSE 2016]
3. How does money solve the problem of 'double coincidence of wants'? What do you mean by demand deposit?
4. What are the two modern forms of money?
5. Define money.
6. Why is currency accepted as a medium of exchange?
7. What is the main source of income of the banks?
8. What do banks do with the money which people deposit in the bank?
9. What is credit?
10. Mention any two terms of credit. [CBSE 2016]

11. What is collateral?
12. Why do banks ask for collateral?
13. State any two informal sources of credit for people of rural India.
14. State any two formal sources of credit for rural India.
15. Who issues currency notes in India?
16. What is barter system?

B. Short answer type questions.

1. What is barter system? Explain with an example.
2. What is the main difficulty of barter system? Explain.
3. How does money eliminate the need for double coincidence of wants? [CBSE 2015]

   OR

   What are the two forms of money? [CBSE 2015]
4. Differentiate between currency and bank money.
5. How does money act as a medium of exchange?

   OR

   "The rupee is widely accepted as a medium of exchange." Explain. [CBSE 2008, 2012, 2013]
6. Why are demand deposits considered as money?
7. How does a bank earn income? Explain.
8. Briefly explain the loan activities of banks.
9. Why do banks maintain cash reserves? [CBSE 2016]
10. What is required to get a loan from a bank? [CBSE 2016]
11. Why are the most credits provided against a collateral security?
12. Why do we need to explain formal sources of credit in India?
13. Why the share of formal sector credit is higher for the richer households compared to the poor households?
14. How are Self-Help Groups (SHGs) the best source to help the poor? [CBSE 2016]
15. Define a cheque. State any two advantages of cheque payments.
16. Why is the supervision in the functioning of formal sources of loans necessary? [CBSE 2016]
17. Why are most of the poor households deprived from the formal sector of loans? [CBSE 2016]

C. Long answer type questions.

1. Define money. How does it function as a medium of exchange?
2. Analyse the role of credit for development.
3. Explain the difference between the formal and informal sectors of credit.
4. Why is it difficult to take loan from formal source, especially for the poor? What value is missing in informal source of credit?
5. Analyse the need to expand the formal sector of credit.
6. Give reasons for emergence of Self-Help Groups (SHGs). How do they function?
7. In what ways, does the Reserve Bank of India supervise the functioning of banks? Why is it necessary?
8. What is SHG? How does it benefit to the members?
9. Why are transactions made in money? What were the shortcomings of the barter system that led to the evolution of money? [CBSE 2016]
10. Mention two sources of credit. Explain with example. [CBSE 2017]

11. Which is the highest banking authority in India? What are its functions? [CBSE 2017]

12. "*Cheap and affordable credit is essential for poor households both in rural and urban areas*". In the light of above statement, explain the social and economic values attached to it? [CBSE 2013]

OR

"*Cheap and affordable credit is crucial for country's development.*" Explain. [CBSE 2011, 2014, 2016]

13. "Credit must be made available to the poor people on appropriate and reasonable terms to respect certain essential values". Explain. [CBSE 2016]

14. Explain the social and economic values for which it is necessary to expand formal sources of credit in India. [CBSE 2016]

15. Name three sources each of formal and informal credit in India. [CBSE 2016]

16. Why do people in rural areas still dependent on informal sources of credit? [CBSE 2016]

17. Differentiate between formal and informal sources of credit. Explain problems faced by borrowers of loan from informal sources. [A.I., Comp. 2013]

OR

What are the two categories of sources of credit? Mention four features of each. [CBSE 2013]

OR

Mention three points of difference between formal sector and informal sector loans. [CBSE 2016]

18. How do banks play an important role in the economy of India? Explain. [CBSE 2015]

OR

"Deposits with the banks are beneficial to the depositors as well as to the nation." Examine the statement. [A.I. 2016]

19. Why is it necessary for the banks and cooperative societies to increase their lending facilities in rural areas? Explain. [CBSE 2015]

OR

Why should the banks and cooperative societies provide more loan facilities to the rural households in India? Give four reasons. [CBSE 2008, 2012]

20. Why are credit arrangements not very fair for all sections of society? Give reasons. Suggest two remedies for the problem. [CBSE 2016]

ANSWERS

MCQS

1. (a)	2. (a)	3. (d)	4. (a)	5. (d)	6. (a)	7. (a)	8. (d)
9. (c)	10. (d)	11. (a)	12. (a)	13. (c)	14. (c)	15. (b)	

Fill in the blanks.

1. Lack of double coincidence of wants
2. Currency
3. Bank money
4. Urban
5. Reserve Bank of India
6. deposits
7. Cooperatives, banks

4

OUTLINE OF THE CHAPTER

At the end of the chapter students will come to know about :

- Production Across Countries
- What is Globalisation?
- Impact of Globalisation on the Indian Economy

Globalisation and the Indian Economy

4.1 PRODUCTION ACROSS COUNTRIES

In today's world, consumers have a wide choices of goods and services. A flood of brands can be seen in all goods and services. When consumers go to the market, they find various models of phones, digital cameras, television sets, shoes, garments, electrical appliances. We find companies offering better quality products to consumers at cheaper rates. Such a variety of goods in Indian markets was not found even two decades ago. In a matter of years, our markets have seen remarkable transformation. How did this transformation take place? What factors are responsible for this kind of change? What are its effects on the Indian economy? These are some of the questions which we shall try to study and analyse in this chapter.

In recent years, multinational companies (MNCs) have come up in a big way. A large number of MNCs are working in our country.

What is meant by an MNC?

An MNC is a large company that owns or controls production and marketing operations in two or more countries.

An MNC is different from other companies. The MNCs set up offices and factories for production in regions where they can get cheap labour and other resources. This is done so that the cost of production is low and the MNCs can earn greater profits. The MNCs do not produce all the goods on their own and at one single place. Its activities are spread across other countries. Consider the following example.

vodafone HYUNDAI Reliance Coca-Cola

Suppose a large MNC produces industrial equipment. The company designs its products from the Research and Development (R&D) centres in the United States of America. Then, it gives orders for the production of components to the manufacturing units located in China as per specified designs. These components are assembled in Mexico and Eastern Europe and the finished products are sold all over the world. Customer care related services of these products are carried out in the call centres located in India.

In the above example, research is carried out in the USA because the country has Research centre and goods are manufactured in China because of cheap manufacturing location. Mexico and Eastern European countries are useful for their closeness to the markets in the USA and Europe. The company has set up company's customer care centre in Bengaluru because India provides cheap skilled engineers and workers. Had the MNC produced the complete product in its own country which ensures a very high salary structure, difficult labour laws, costly land and limited human capital, the cost of production would have been 3–4 times higher. In this way, MNCs not only sell their products globally but also produce them globally.

Features of MNCs

- The parent company of an MNC is located in one country and its subsidiaries are working in many countries.
- Most MNCs are of giant size. They have huge capital base.
- The MNCs have advanced technology.
- MNCs are different from other companies. Their activities are spread across the countries while other companies are local in their existence.

Interlinking Production Across Countries

Generally, MNCs have set up production units where

(a) it is close to the markets.
(b) skilled and unskilled labour is available at low cost.
(c) the availability of other factors of production is assured.
(d) government policies look after their interests.

After considering all the above-mentioned factors, MCNs set up their factories and offices for production.

The money spent by MNCs on the purchase of assets such as land, buildings, machines and more equipments is called **investment** from the point of view of MNCs. Investment made by MNCs in other countries is called **foreign investment**.

Three Different Ways of Investment by MNCs

There are mainly three ways by which MNCs are spreading and interlinking productions. These are discussed below.

1. Join Ventures. Of different countries, MNCs may prefer to set up production jointly with some of the local companies. Local companies are benefitted in two ways :

- *First*, MNCs can provide money for additional investments like buying new machines for faster production.
- *Second*, MNCs might bring with them the latest technology for production.

2. Taking Over Local Companies. The most common route for MNC investments is to buy up local companies and then to expand production. The MNCs with huge capital base can quite easily do so.

For example, Cargill Foods, an American MNC, has taken over Parakh Foods, an Indian company. Cargill has taken over all the four oil refineries of Parakh Foods and thus has become the largest producer of edible oils in India. Similarly, Thums Up of Parle Group was taken over by Coca Cola.

3. Placing Orders. There is another way in which MNCs control production. Large MNCs in developed countries place orders for production with small producers and then sell them under their own brand names after some quality checks and improvements. For example, garment, footwear, sport items, etc., are produced by a large number of small producers around the world on behalf of MNCs. These products are produced by the MNCs and then MNCs sell them under their brand name all over the world.

In India if you see carefully on the labels, many of the goods sold under names of American companies are made in China, many garments of European brands are made in Bangladesh and many Japanese brands are made in Korea.

Thus, we see that there are a variety of ways in which the MNCs are spreading their production either through merger of companies or through joint ventures or placing supply orders to the small producers of different countries. In this way MNCs play the role in interlinking production across countries.

Foreign Trade and Integration of Markets

Like production, trade is also expanding. Foreign trade connects different countries with each other. It provides opportunities to the domestic producers to sell their products in other countries. Now producers produce and sell not only in domestic markets but they go and complete in other countries' market also. Similarly, domestic consumers can buy goods produced in other countries. Thus, foreign trade provides a greater choice to buy goods. For example, people in the United Kingdom can buy mangoes grown in India. Mobile phones produced in China can be sold in India and Indian cotton textiles can be sold in the American markets.

Foreign trade, thus, facilitates selling a product in a market beyond the boundaries of the country where it is produced.

DID YOU KNOW?

Foreign Trade. When trade takes place with other countries it is called foreign trade. Normally this term is used when produce of one country is sold to another country.

International Trade. It is a more complex form of trade. It involves activities relating to production and trade of goods and services across the countries.

GLOSSARY

Multinational Companies : A multinational company (MNC) is a large company that owns and controls operations in two or more countries.

Globalisation : It is a process by which a domestic economy gets integrated with the rest of the world through trade, capital flows, spread of technology.

Research and development : It refers to innovative activities undertaken by corporations or governments in developing new services or products, or improving existing services or products.

Investment : An investment is a monetary asset purchased with the idea that the asset will provide income in the future or will later be sold at a higher price for a profit.

Foreign investment : Foreign investment means investment made by a MNC in foreign countries.

Skilled labour : Skilled labour is a segment of the workforce that has specialised know-how, training, and experience to carry out more complex physical, or mental tasks than routine job functions.

Unskilled labour : Unskilled labour refers to workers who have no special training or experience.

LET'S RECAPITULATE

- An MNC is a large company that owns or controls production and marketing operations in two or more countries. It is different from other companies which are local in existence.
- MNCs set up offices and factories for production in regions where they can get cheap labour and other resources.
- The parent company of an MNC is located in one country and its subsidiaries are working in many countries.
- There are mainly three ways by which MNCs are spreading and interlinking productions, i.e., joint ventures, taking over local companies and placing orders.
- Foreign trade connects different countries and provides opportunities to the domestic producers to sell their products to other countries.
- Foreign trade facilitates selling a product in a market beyond the boundaries of the country where it is produced.

CHECK YOUR UNDERSTANDING

1. What is an MNC?

   OR

   How would you say Coca Cola is an MNC?
2. Why do MNCs set up their production centres at different places?
3. How do MNCs increase their profits?
4. In what ways an MNC different from other companies?
5. What do you understand by the term investment?
6. What is foreign investment?
7. What are the considerations that are taken into account by an MNC while setting up production units in other countries?

4.2 WHAT IS GLOBALISATION?

Today's world is now turning into one large group of economies called the global economy. During the past 20–30 years, the MNCs have been increasingly looking for locations around the world which would be cheap for their production. Foreign investment by MNCs in these countries has been rising. At the same time, foreign trade between countries has been rising rapidly.

Meaning of Globalisation

As studied earlier, the MNCs have helped in the integration of production and markets across countries. This has been termed as *globalisation.*

Globalisation can, thus, be defined as the process of rapid integration or inter-connection between economies of different countries. In recent years, there is increasing movement of goods and services among different countries. Globalisation results in free flow of goods and services, technology and human resource across the countries.

The MNCs not only produce goods but a sizeable part of foreign trade is also controlled by them. For example, Ford Motors in India not only produces cars for the Indian markets, but also exports cars to other developing countries and exports car components for its many factories around the world. Similarly, activities of most MNCs involve substantial trade in goods and also services.

Factors Enabling Globalisation

The two main factors that led to the development of globalisation are discussed below.

- **Technology.** Past improvement in technology has been one of the major factors contributing to globalisation.

  Technology has stimulated the globalisation process most. It has enabled the globalisation process in the following ways :

  (a) Improvement in the trasportation technology has made faster delivery of goods across long distances possible and that too at lower cost.

  (b) Improvement in information and telecommunication technology has proved more remarkable. The invention and the use of computers, internet, mobile phones, fax, etc., have made contact with each other around the world quite easy. Now we may have access to any information within no time.

  (c) Information and communication technology has also played a crucial role in spreading out production of their services. For example, a news magazine for London readers can be printed in New Delhi with the help of Internet technology.

- **Liberalisation.** *Liberalisation implies liberating trade and industry from unwanted government controls and restrictions.*

Next to technology, liberalisation has played a crucial role for promoting globalisation. Global production and trade are greatly promoted by liberalisation, that is, removal of tariffs, capital controls and other state imposed restrictions on the movement of resources between nations. Globalisation requires supporting regulatory frameworks. Relaxation in tax laws, labour legislation and environmental codes can greatly encourage global investment.

Liberalisation Measures in India

In the early years of planning, India imposed barriers on foreign trade and foreign investment. This policy was based on the belief that such types of restrictions are necessary to protect the interests of domestic producers. Further, India wanted to become self-reliant due to which it promoted investments in public sector undertakings. The government took following measures to promote liberalisation.

(i) **Lifting of Trade Barriers.** Since 1991, the government decided that competition with foreign producers would improve the performance of domestic producers.

The policy of liberalisation is also known as the New Economic Policy (NEP) because the government has taken a U-turn in its policy that remained in course for more than four decades.

Thus, barriers on foreign trade and foreign investment were removed to a large extent. This meant that goods could be imported and exported easily and also foreign companies could set up factories and offices here.

(a) These barriers were removed because India wanted to integrate the economy with other countries.

(b) The removal of barriers were sought to achieve rapid economic development of the country.

(c) Government wanted Indian industry to compete with foreign companies.

(ii) **Special Economic Zones.** As a result of liberalisation of trade and investment, the government of India established several **Special Economic Zones (SEZs)** where world class infrastructural facilities like electricity, roads, transport, storage, water, recreational and educational facilities were made available to foreign companies. Moreover, those foreign companies who set up their units in such economic zones are provided relaxation in taxes for an initial period of 5 years.

Trade Barriers

Trade barriers refer to the policies which restrict free trade to protect domestic industries/producers from foreign competition. Imposing import duties (i.e., tax on import of goods) or quantitative restrictions on foreign goods are called trade barriers.

How Trade Barriers Protect Domestic Industries?

For example, suppose Government of India imposes import duty (called tax barrier) on Chinese toys. Due to this import duty, the price of Chinese toys in Indian market would increase and hence the import of toys from China would come down. This would protect Indian toy manufacturers. Similarly, quotas (i.e., quantitative restrictions) can be fixed for the import of certain goods.

(iii) **Flexibility in Labour Laws.** Foreign companies were allowed flexibility in labour laws so that they could employ workers for short periods (on temporary basis) and hence, cut-off the cost of production. Employer has not to give social security benefits to workers such as gratuity. Companies can exploit the conditions of surplus labour and hence can pay minimum wages.

(iv) **Make in India.** Recently the Government has launched a massive programme called 'Make in India' inviting foreign investors to come to India and utilise the potential of cheap labour and land costs to set up industry. The foreign investors are being offered incentives to invest in India.

World Trade Organisation

World Trade Organisation (WTO) is an international body under the United Nations. It was set up in 1995 to promote trade among member countries. Its headquarter is located in Geneva (Switzerland). India became its member on January 1, 1995. Presently there are 164 member countries of this organisation. All the member countries are required to adopt laws and policies in order to comply with the WTO rules.

Foreign Trade – An important Component of Globalisation

- Foreign trade implies exchange of goods and services across the countries. Hence, it is an important component of globalisation.

- Foreign trade helps to expand the size of market for producers across the countries.
- It works to integrate market globally.

Functions of WTO

The WTO was set up to perform the following functions :

(i) Monitoring WTO trade agreements

(ii) Handling of trade disputes

(iii) Providing technical assistance and training to developing countries and

(iv) To co-operate with other international organisations.

Objectives of WTO

The main objectives of WTO are as follows :

(i) To promote multilateral trade, i.e., trade among many nations.

(ii) Progressive liberalisation and elimination of tariffs and other barriers to trade in goods as well as services.

(iii) To promote world trade so that every member country is benefitted.

(iv) To expand and utilise world resources in the most optimum manner.

(v) To enhance competition among all trading partners so as to benefit the consumers.

Though WTO is supposed to allow free trade for all, in practice, it is seen that the developed countries have unfairly retained trade barriers. On the other hand, WTO rules have forced the developing countries to remove trade barriers. For example in USA, farmers get huge sums of money from the government for production and for exports to other countries. Due to this, farmers are able to sell their products at very low prices to other countries. However, developing countries have lifted trade barriers as per WTO rules. Thus WTO is not fair to developing countries.

Steps needed to be taken

(i) Rules and regulations should be uniform for all the countries.

(ii) Ensure that the developed countries do not retain trade barriers unfairly.

(iii) Labour laws should be implemented properly.

GLOSSARY

Global economy : It refers to all the economies of the world, considered as one unit.

Technology : It refers to methods, systems and devices which are the result of scientific knowledge being used for practical purposes.

Liberalisation : The loosening of government control in a country when private sector companies start working with fewer restrictions and government allows private players to expand for the growth of the country.

Trade barrier : It is a government imposed hurdle in the way of free flow of goods and services. These hurdles include: tax on import, fixing quota, licensing etc.

World Trade Organisation : WTO is a forum where governments of various member nations negotiate the trade agreements and deal with the regulation of trade between the nations.

LET'S RECAPITULATE

- Globalisation is the process of rapid integration or inter-connection between economies of different countries.
- Globalisation results in free flow of goods and services, capital, technology and labour across the countries.
- Two main factors that led to the development of globalisation are technology and liberalisation.
- Liberalisation means liberating trade and industry from unwanted government controls and restrictions.
- For liberalisation the government took following measures :

  (i) Lifting of trade barriers

  (ii) Setting up Special Economic Zones

  (iii) Providing flexibility in labour laws

  (iv) Promoting 'Make in India' programme

- World Trade Organisation (WTO) is an international body under the United Nations and it was set up in 1995 to promote trade among member countries.
- Though WTO is supposed to allow free trade for all, in practice, it is seen that the developed countries have unfairly retained trade barriers.

CHECK YOUR UNDERSTANDING

1. What are trade barriers?
2. What do you understand by tariffs?
3. How can quota be used as a trade barrier?
4. What is the basic aim of WTO?
5. Fill in the blanks :

   WTO was started at the initiative of the ________ countries. The aim of the WTO is to liberalise ________ trade. At present ________ countries of the world are members of the WTO. In practice, the ________ countries have unfairly retained trade ________. On the other hand, WTO rules have forced the ________ countries to remove trade barriers.
6. What do you think can be done so that trade between countries is more fair?

   OR

   How can trade be made fair between the countries?

4.3 IMPACT OF GLOBALISATION ON THE INDIAN ECONOMY

Let us now evaluate the impacts of globalisation on the Indian economy under the following two heads.

Positive Impacts

(i) **Technology.** Modern technologies and management services are being provided by MNCs in India.

(ii) **Inflow of Foreign Capital.** The inflow of foreign currency in the country has increased as MNCs bring capital in foreign currency.

(iii) **Competition.** The entry of MNCs has promoted competition in the domestic market. This has proved very beneficial for the Indian companies as well as consumers. Tata Motors, Infosys, Ranbaxy, Asian Paints and Sundaram Fastners are some of the Indian companies which have benefitted from the increased competition. Globalisation has also helped these large Indian companies to emerge as multinationals. These MNCs have expanded their business globally creating employment opportunities for Indian people abroad. They earn valuable foreign exchange.

(iv) **Benefits to Consumers.**
- We have a wide variety of goods and services before us in the market.
- The latest models of the digital cameras, mobile phones and televisions made by leading manufacturers of the world are available in the market.
- Today, Indians are buying cars produced by nearly all the top companies in the world.
- A similar explosion of brands can be seen for many other goods.

(v) **New Employment Opportunities.** Outsourcing has emerged as a major business acitivity. In outsourcing, a company hires regular service from external sources, mostly from other countries, which was previously provided internally or within the country. Because of the growth of the fast modes of communication, particularly the growth of information technology, many of the services like voice-based business processes [popularly known as **BPO** (Business Process Outsourcing) or **call centres**], record keeping, accountancy, banking services, etc., are being outsourced by companies in developed countries to India. With reasonable degree of skill and accuracy, India is capable of providing these services at a cheaper cost.

Thus globalisation has created new employment opportunities in the country.

Negative Impacts

(i) Standards of living have improved only in urban areas. It has increased the income and quality of consumption of only high income groups. Poverty is still widespread in the country.

(ii) The growth has been concentrated only in some selected areas in the service sector such as telecommunication, information technology, finance, entertainment, travel and hospitality services, real estate and trade. Globalisation has bypassed the agricultural sector which provides livelihoods to millions of people in the country.

(iii) Although employment opportunities have been created at the upper end (e.g., technologists, management personnels, engineers, etc.) but they are missing at the lower end, i.e., for unskilled persons.

The Struggle for a Fair Globalisation

The above-mentioned positive and negative impacts indicate that globalisation has not benefitted everyone. The best use of new opportunities has been made mostly by people having education, skill and wealth. Thus, it is very important to have fair globalisation to create opportunities for all and also to ensure that the benefits of globalisation are shared better. Government policies must protect the interests of all the people of the country.

Government should ensure that labour laws are properly implemented and the workers get their rights. Small producers should be supported to improve their performance till they become strong enough to compete.

Besides this, the government can use trade and investment barriers and can also negotiate at the WTO for 'fairer rules'. Along with other developing countries, it can fight against the domination of developed countries in the WTO.

GLOSSARY

Capital : Capital investment is a sum acquired by a company to further its business objectives.

Outsourcing : It is the business practice of hiring a party outside a company to perform services and create goods that traditionally were performed in-house by the company's own employees and staff.

Communication : Communications are the systems and processes that are used to communicate or broadcast information, especially by means of electricity or radio waves.

Consumers : Consumers are the people or organisations that purchase products or services.

LET'S RECAPITULATE

- The impacts of globalisation on the Indian economy are both positive and negative.
- Positive impacts include, modern technology, inflow of foreign capital, competition, benefits to consumers, new employment opportunities etc.
- Consumers get variety of goods with latest models of the digital cameras, mobile phones, televisions, etc.
- Outsourcing has emerged as a major business activity
- Negative impacts include, improved standard of living only in urban areas, growth concentrated in selected areas and employment opportunities missing at lower end.

CHECK YOUR UNDERSTANDING

1. Define outsourcing.
2. How has the entry of MNCs benefitted the consumers?
3. Name some Indian companies that have emerged as multinationals.
4. Why do governments try to attract more foreign investment?
5. How globalisation has posed major challenges for a large number of small producers?

EXERCISES

I. A. Multiple choice questions.

Choose the correct answers.

1. Globalisation shall result in [CBSE 2011]
   (a) lesser competition among producers (b) greater competition among producers
   (c) greater competition among buyers (d) destruction of large-scale producers
2. The most common route for investments by MNCs in countries around the world is to [CBSE 2011]
   (a) set up new factories
   (b) buy existing local companies
   (c) form partnership with local companies
   (d) none of these
3. Which one of the following is a major benefit of joint production between a local company and multinational company? [CBSE 2011]
   (a) MNC can bring latest technology in the production.
   (b) MNC can control the increase in price.
   (c) MNC can buy the local company.
   (d) MNC can sell the products under their brand name.
4. Tax on imports is an example of [CBSE 2011]
   (a) Terms of trade (b) Collateral (c) Trade barriers (d) Foreign trade
5. Removing barriers or restrictions set by the government is known as [CBSE 2011]
   (a) globalisation (b) privatisation (c) liberalisation (d) fair trade practice
6. Effect of Chinese toys on Indian toy market is [CBSE 2011]
   (a) no effect (b) making profit (c) suffering from losses (d) none of these
7. Which one of the following is not true regarding impact of globalisation in India? [CBSE 2011]
   (a) It has created jobs in the service sector.
   (b) People with education, skill and wealth have not been benefitted.
   (c) Benefits of globalisation are not shared equally.
   (d) Labour laws are not implemented properly and workers are denied of their rights.
8. How many countries are currently the members of the World Trade Organisation? [CBSE 2011]
   (a) 164 (b) 250 (c) 230 (d) 140
9. Which of the following is a 'barrier' of foreign trade? [CBSE 2013]
   (a) Tax on exports (b) Tax on imports (c) Tax on local trade (d) High income tax
10. Which one of the following was the main aim to form 'World Trade Organisation'? [CBSE 2013]
    (a) To liberalise international trade (b) To promote trade of rich countries
    (c) To promote trade of poor countries (d) To promote bilateral trade

11. Why did the government decide to remove barriers on foreign trade and foreign competitors?
(a) To earn the foreign exchange
(b) To compete with producers in the world market
(c) To bring faster growth in the economy
(d) All of these

12. Ranbaxy is a multinational company which is associated with
(a) automobiles
(b) cell phones
(c) medicines
(d) none of these

13. Which of the following companies is an example of Indian MNC?
(a) Tata Motors
(b) Infosys
(c) Ranbaxy
(d) All of these

14. The MNCs generally select those regions for setting up their factories where
(a) It is close to the market.
(b) Trained skilled labour is available.
(c) Government policies look after their interest.
(d) All of these

B. Match the following items given in Column A with those in Column B. Choose the correct answer from the options given below.

1.

	Column A		Column B
A.	A company whose activities are spread across the countries	(i)	Ranbaxy
B.	An Indian MNC associated with automobiles	(ii)	MNC
C.	An Indian MNC associated with medicines	(iii)	Joint Ventures
D.	A way of investment by MNC	(iv)	Tata Motors

Mark the correct option.
(a) (iv)-(i)-(iii)-(ii)
(b) (ii)-(iv)-(i)-(iii)
(c) (iii)-(ii)-(iv)-(i)
(d) (i)-(iv)-(iii)-(ii)

2.

	Column A		Column B
A.	Integration of production and markets across countries	(i)	July 1991
B.	Factor enabling globalisation	(ii)	Tax on import
C.	New Economic Policy	(iii)	Advancements in technology
D.	A trade barrier	(iv)	Globalisation

Mark the correct option.
(a) (ii)-(i)-(iii)-(iv)
(b) (iii)-(iv)-(ii)-(i)
(c) (ii)-(iii)-(i)-(iv)
(d) (iv)-(iii)-(i)-(ii)

C. Fill in the blanks.

1. Removing barriers or restrictions from foreign trade is called ______________.
2. The WTO was established in ______________.
3. The head office of WTO is located in ______________.
4. Obtaining goods and services from outside sources is called ______________.
5. The investment made by MNCs in foreign countries is called ______________.
6. Total membership of WTO is ______________ countries.
7. The most common route for MNC investments is to buy up ______________.

D. Correct the following statements and rewrite.

(i) In an MNC production is organised in a simple way.
(ii) In the competition between Indian and Chinese toys, Indian toys prove better.
(iii) The main channel connecting countries in the past was communication.

(iv) Liberalisation is the process of slow integration or interconnection between countries.
(v) Slow improvement in technology has been one minor factor that has stimulated the globalisation process.
(vi) Tax on exports is an example of trade barrier.

E. In the question given below, there are two statements marked as Assertion (A) and Reason (R). Read the statements and chose the correct option:

Assertion (A) : In the past two or three decades, more and more MNCs have been looking for locations around the world which would be cheap for their production.

Reason (R) : Foreign trade results in connecting the markets in different countries.

Options:

(a) Both A and R are true and R is the correct explanation of A.
(b) Both A and R are true but R is not the correct explanation of A.
(c) A is correct but R is wrong.
(d) A is wrong but R is correct.

F. State whether the following statement is true or false :

Government has allowed flexibility in labour laws to attract foreign investment.

II. A. Very short answer type questions.

1. What is meant by liberalisation?
2. State two factors that have enabled globalisation.
3. What is meant by trade barrier? [CBSE 2015]
4. What do you mean by liberalisation?
5. Which organisation lays stress on liberalisation of foreign trade and foreign investment? [CBSE 2014]
6. What is the full form of WTO?
7. What is meant by MNC?
8. What is foreign investment? [CBSE 2017]
9. Suggest one way which can promote foreign investment in India.
10. What is Special Economic Zone (SEZ)?
11. What is the basic aim of WTO?
12. Why do MNCs set up their offices and factories in those regions where they get cheap labour and other resources? [*CBSE 2016*]

B. Short answer type questions.

1. Differentiate between investment and foreign investment.
2. State two major positive impacts of globalisation on the Indian economy.
3. Why do countries impose trade barriers?
4. Why did government remove trade barriers?
5. What factors affect the decision of an MNC regarding the location of its production units in a particular country?
6. What is MNC? Why do you call Ford Motors an MNC?
7. What is WTO? Write its two functions. [CBSE 2017]
8. How did 'Cargill Foods' become the largest producer of edible oils in India? Explain. [CBSE 2014]
9. How do MNCs help in the growth of local companies? [CBSE 2016]

   OR

   How does Indian MNCs benefit the people in the country? Explain. [CBSE 2017]
10. If the government removes barriers or restrictions set by itself, write what is government actually doing? [CBSE 2016]
11. How do MNCs help in the growth of the local companies? [CBSE 2011, 13]

12. How is production getting interlinked through MNCs? [CBSE 2016]

13. In what ways is a MNC different from other companies? Explain. [CBSE 2015]

14. Where do MNCs set up their production units? [CBSE 2016]

C. Long answer type questions.

1. What do you understand by liberalisation of foreign trade? How has it stimulated the process of globalisation?

   OR

   Liberalisaton of foreign trade and foreign investment has helped the process of globalisation. Explain this statement.

2. What is outsourcing? How does an MNC take advantage of outsourcing? Explain with an example.
3. How has Information Technology (IT) helped the process of globalisation? Explain.
4. What are the various ways in which MNCs set up or control production in other countries?
5. "A wide ranging choice of goods are available in the Indian markets." Support the statement with examples in context of globalisation. [CBSE 2016]
6. How has globalisation been advantageous to both the producers as well as the consumers in India? [CBSE 2012, 2014, 2016]
7. What is globalisation? Mention any two positive or two negative impacts of globalisation on trade. [CBSE 2017]
8. In recent years, how our markets have been transformed? Explain with examples. [CBSE 2014, 15]
9. How are MNCs controlling and spreading their production across countries? Explain with examples. [CBSE 2015]

   OR

   Explain by giving examples that Multinational Corporations (MNCs) are spreading their production in different ways. [CBSE 2016]

10. Supposing you find two persons arguing. One is saying globalisation has hurt our country's development. The other is telling globalisation is helping India develop. How would you respond to these arguments? [CBSE 2018]
11. What are the steps taken by the Indian government to attract foreign investment? [CBSE 2016]
12. Should more Indian companies emerge as MNCs? How would it benefit the people in the countries? [CBSE 2011]
13. What steps should be taken to make trade more fair between the countries? [CBSE 2016]

ANSWERS

MCQS

1. (b)	2. (b)	3. (a)	4. (c)	5. (c)	6. (c)	7. (b)	8. (a)
9. (b)	10. (a)	11. (d)	12. (c)	13. (a)	14. (d)		

Fill in the blanks.

1. liberalisation	2. 1995	3. Geneva (Switzerland)
4. outsourcing	5. foreign investment	6. 164
7. Local industries		

5

Consumer Rights

OUTLINE OF THE CHAPTER

At the end of the chapter students will come to know about :

- The Consumer in the Market Place
- Consumer Movement
- Consumer Rights

5.1 THE CONSUMER IN THE MARKET PLACE

We are all consumers. When we pay a price for a commodity or service and use it, we become consumers. Anyone who buys goods and services for his/her use is a consumer.

Sometimes the seller cheats us as he or she gives poor quality goods, or charges more for a commodity or service. What should we do in such cases? In this chapter, we will study about how consumers are exploited. What are the ways in which they can exercise their rights as consumers to get a fair deal from the sellers? What are the duties of consumers while buying anything from the market? What the government is doing to protect their interests?

Participation in the Market

- We participate in the market both as producers and consumers.
- As producers of goods and services we could be working in any of the sectors such as agriculture, industry, or services.
- As consumers we participate in the market when we purchase goods and services that we need. These are the final goods that people as consumers use.

In the past, the general belief was *leave the consumer to himself,* i.e., a consumer is the best judge of his own interests, let him decide for himself. But with the growing commercialisation and marketisation, it was realised that a consumer stands at a much weaker footing than a seller. A seller can always manipulate the market conditions to his favour. Hence, it is essential to protect a consumer against exploitation at the hands of the sellers.

Consumer protection is important for the following reasons :

(i) To make sure that producers and sellers do not adopt unfair trade practices.

(ii) To encourage and ensure effective implementation of consumer protection laws.

(iii) To check anti-social activities like hoarding, black marketing, etc.

(iv) To protect the small borrowers from the moneylenders who force them to sell their land or products to them to pay back the amount of loan.

(v) To prevent exploitation of labourers who work in the unorganised sector.

Therefore, consumer should be protected in the market place. Hence, rules and regulations are required in the market place.

Different Ways of Consumer's Exploitation

We have a variety of goods available in the market. Our demand for goods and services is influenced by the advertisements in television, newspapers and magazines. When we, as consumers, do not have sufficient information about the products, we usually get exploited and are sometimes even harassed by the business community.

Some common ways by which consumers are exploited by manufacturers and traders are mentioned below.

(i) **Underweight and Undermeasurement :** The goods being sold in the market are sometimes not measured or weighed correctly.

(ii) **High Prices :** Very often the traders charge a price higher than the prescribed retail price.

(iii) **Substandard Quality :** The goods sold are sometimes of substandard quality. Selling of medicines beyond their expiry dates and supply of defective home appliances are generally the regular grievances of consumers.

In the name of genuine parts or goods, fake or duplicate items are being sold to the consumers. This is called an *act of deception*.

(iv) **Adulterated Products :** Adulteration means mixing inferior quality goods with superior products. In edible items such as oil, ghee and spices adulteration is made in order to earn higher profits. This causes financial and health loss to the consumer. We have heard about people dying because of adulterated wine.

Examples :

- Adding wheat flour to milk.
- Adding sand or crushed stones to foodgrain to increase the weight.
- Mixing of used tea leaves with original tea leaves.
- Mixing vanaspati with pure ghee.

(v) **Misleading and False Information :** Companies spend a huge amount on advertisements to attract customers. By giving misleading or false information, these large and powerful companies succeed in cheating the consumers who buy goods in small amounts and are scattered. These companies manipulate the market. For example,

- A company sold powdered milk for babies all over the world claiming that its product is better than mother's milk. But that is not true.
- Similarly, a long battle had been fought in courts to make cigarette manufacturing companies accept that their product could cause cancer.

(vi) **Lack of Safety Devices :** In order to increase the sale of their products, some producers especially of electrical goods, electronic devices and such other appliances, try to produce things of poor quality without caring for the standard safeguard norms. Such things prove very dangerous for the customers and some are even involved in serious accidents.

(vii) **Artificial Scarcity :** In order to get more and more profit, certain unscrupulous traders resort to hoarding of things thereby creating artificial scarcity. They sell these things later on at higher prices.

(viii) **Poor After-sale Services :** Many of the high cost durable items, such as electrical or electronic equipments, home appliances and cars, etc., need adequate after-sale care. The supplier does not provide the satisfactory after-sale services despite the necessary payments.

GLOSSARY

Consumer	:	Consumer is a person who buys goods and services for the satisfaction of his/her wants.
Producer	:	Producer is a person who manufactures or sells goods and services.
Consumer exploitation	:	It is a situation in which consumer is cheated by the producer.
Consumer protection	:	Protection of consumer's right against wrong practices of sellers in the market is called consumer protection.

LET'S RECAPITULATE

- With the growing commercialisation and marketisation, it was realised that a consumer stands at a much weaker footing than a seller.
- It is essential to protect a consumer against exploitation at the hands of the sellers.
- We participate in the market both as producers and consumers.
- When consumers do not have sufficient information about the products, they usually get exploited and are sometimes even harassed by the business community.
- Some common ways by which consumers get exploited are, underweight and under-measurement, high prices, substandard quality products, adulterated products, misleading and false information, lack of safety devices, artificial scarcity, poor after-sale services, etc.

CHECK YOUR UNDERSTANDING

1. How do the large companies often manipulate the market? Give an example.
2. Why are rules and regulations required in the market place?
3. How are consumers exploited in the market place?
4. Who are producers and consumers? Give examples.

5.2 CONSUMER MOVEMENT

Need for Consumer Movement

The need for consumer movement arose out as dissatisfactions of the consumers because of the following reasons :

- Sellers were used to indulge in unfair trade practices.
- There was no legal system available to protect the consumers.
- When a consumer was not happy with a particular brand product or shop, it was assumed that it was the responsibility of the consumers to be careful while purchasing a commodity or service.
- The only way available to consumers was not to go to the shop, not to buy that brand, if they are cheated.

Consumer Movement in India

In the 1960s and 1970s as education levels in the masses improved, people realised that they should not be cheated. Thus it all began as 'social force' with the aim to protect and promote consumer interests against unfair and unethical trade practices.

Till the 1970s, consumer organisations were largely engaged in writing articles and holding exhibitions. They formed consumer groups to look into the malpractices in ration shops and over-crowding in the road passenger transport.

- More recently, India witnessed an upsurge in the number of consumer groups. This is because of more and more cases of consumer exploitation by the private traders.
- The activities of various **Consumer Forums** forced the government to enact the Consumer Protection Act 1986, popularly known as COPRA.

National Consumer Day in India in celebrated on 24th December every year. On this day, the Consumer Protection Act, 1986 had received the assent of the President.

Reasons for Consumer's Exploitation

The following are the major reasons that cause exploitation of the consumers :

(i) **Lack of Information :** In a free market economy, producers and sellers are free to produce any goods or services in any quantity and there is no regulation on the prices. In such cases, providing full and correct information about the product to consumers is of great importance. In the absence of information about different aspects of the products namely, price, quality, composition, conditions of use, terms of purchase, etc., the consumers are liable to make a wrong decision and hence lose money.

(ii) **Shortage of Goods and Services :** The consumers are exploited when the goods and services are not available in the required quantity or numbers. Limited supplies are a result, usually, of lower production of goods, as compared to the demand. This gives rise to tendency of hoarding and price increase.

(iii) **Limited Competition :** In some cases, single producer or a group of producers controls the production and supply of a product. He is in a position to restrict the availability of supplies. There is, thus, a possibility of manipulation in prices and availability.

(iv) **Illiteracy :** Illiteracy is one of the major reasons that lead to exploitation of consumers. The level of consumer consciousness in our country is generally low. The level of illiteracy directly affects the level of awareness about products and the markets.

(v) **Ill-effects of Advertisements :** Most of the customers are so much attracted by the advertisement of different articles that they do not try to verify the quality of those goods. They buy with a lightning speed and often repent afterwards.

GLOSSARY

Free market : It is a system in which the prices for goods and services are self-regulated by the open market, based on supply and demand, with little or no government control.

Hoarding : The practice of collecting or accumulating something, such as money or food.

Demand : The quantity of a commodity that a consumer is willing to purchase at a certain price.

Supply : The total amount of a product (good or service) that a seller is willing to offer at any specified price.

LET'S RECAPITULATE

- The need for consumer movement arose out because of the dissatisfaction of the consumers in the market.
- The activities of various Consumer Forums forced the government to enact the Consumer Protection Act 1986, popularly known as COPRA.
- In India, the National Consumer Day is celebrated every year on 24th December.
- The major reasons that cause exploitation of the consumers are, lack of information, shortage of goods and services, limited competition, illiteracy, ill-effects of advertisements, etc.

CHECK YOUR UNDERSTANDING

1. When was Consumer Protection Act enacted in India?
2. Which day is observed as National Consumer Day?
3. Consumer movement originated as social force in India. Explain the statement.

5.3 CONSUMER RIGHTS

Consumer rights refer to the legal rights which are given to the consumers to protect themselves against wrong practices of sellers in the market. They are the obligations sellers have to fulfil for selling a product as service to the consumers like safety of the product, right price, etc.

Consumer protection covers

(a) Physical protection of consumers against unsafe products,

(b) Economic protection against unfair trade practices and

(c) Protection of public interest against monopolistic and restrictive trade practices.

Consumers of today enjoy the following rights as provided by the Indian Laws :

1. **Right to be Informed.** *Right to be informed means the right of information about the quality, quantity of the product, etc.* All the consumers have the 'Right to be Informed' about the particulars of goods and services that they purchase. They have the right to be informed about the quality, quantity, potency, purity, standard and price of goods. Consumers can then complain and ask for compensation or replacement if the product proves to be defective in any manner.

   Examples :

   (i) If people sell medicines that have expired severe action can be taken against them.

   (ii) Consumer can complain if someone sells a good at more than the maximum retail price printed on the product.

In recent times, the Right to Information has been expanded through **Right to Information (RTI) Act.** In October 2005, the Government of India enacted a law, popularly known as RTI Act, which ensures the citizens all the information about the functioning of government departments.

Consumer Movement : A Global History

Though the consumer movement made its appearance in England after the Second World War, its real beginning was in 1962 when a declaration about the consumer rights was made in America. At that time, four basic consumer rights viz., right to choose, right to information, right to safety and right to be heard were recognised. **Ralph Nadar**, a consumer activists is considered as a *Father of Consumer Movement.* March 15 is now celebrated as the **World Consumer Rights Day**. In 1985, certain guidelines were laid down to achieve the objectives of maintaining protection for consumers and to establish high level ethical conduct for those engaged in production and distribution of goods and services. These UN guidelines were adopted by the United Nations in 1985.

This was a tool for nations to adopt measures to protect consumers and for consumer advocacy groups to press their governments to do so.

DID YOU KNOW?

Consumer Awareness : Consumer's consciousness towards his/her rights and duties is known as consumer awareness. The knowledge of the consumers towards their rights and protection is called consumer awareness. There is a need for consumer awareness because sellers may exploit them, if they are not conscious.

Consumer Education : Consumer education means making consumers aware of their right and duties.

2. **Right to Choose.** Under Consumer Protection Act (COPRA), a consumer has the right to choose the good among a variety of goods which he/she likes. This right is granted to the consumers to ensure that they can buy, as per their choice. They cannot be forced to buy a thing what they do not like.

   Examples :

   (i) A student wants to purchase a pen, the stationer says that he can sell the pen only if you buy also exercise book for which you are not interested.

   (ii) Sometimes LPG gas supply dealers insist that you have to buy the stove from them when you take a new connection.

In both the cases, consumer's right to choice is denied.

3. **Right to Seek Redressal.**

   - Consumers have the right to seek redressal against unfair trade practices and exploitation. If any damage is done to a consumer, he has the right to get compensation depending upon the degree of damage.
   - There is a need to provide an easy and effective public system by which this can be done.

   Example :

   Suppose Geeta – a housewife buys an air conditioner for ₹40,000. After sometimes she finds it unfunctional. Then, she can register its complain in the company about defect. If the company fails to provide her necessary service, then she is cheated by the company. She has a right to ask the company for refund of her money or replace the defective air-conditioner with the new one.

4. **Right to Safety.** The consumers have the right to be protected against marketing of goods and services, which are hazardous to life and property.
5. **Right to be Heard.** The consumer's interests should receive due considerations at appropriate forums relating to consumer welfare.

The COPRA has empowered the consumer to represent the case himself and there is no requirement to hire a lawyer for representing his/her case in the consumer court. Therefore, even the poorest consumer can represent his/her case.

However, consumers are reluctant to seek redressal because

(i) they do not know the procedure to file complaint.
(ii) often, they have to hire a lawyer and fees has to be paid to them.
(iii) takes long time to get justice.

Consumer Protection Act, 1986

This Act was passed by the government in 1986 for the protection of the consumer's rights which is known as COPRA. It is one of the most important legal measures in protecting the rights of the consumers. The Act came into force with effect from 1st July 1987. The Act was amended in 1991, 1993 and 2002.

Main Features of COPRA

Following are the main features of Consumer Protection Act :

(i) The Act applies to all goods and services.
(ii) It covers all the sectors whether public, private or co-operative societies.
(iii) It provides the rights to the consumers, which include : (a) Right to be informed, (b) Right to choose, (c) Right to seek redressal, (d) Right to safety and (e) Right to be heard.
(iv) Most important feature of this Act is the provision for setting up a *three-tier system*, popularly known as consumer courts at national, state and district levels. At national level, it is called the **National Consumer Commission** which is the apex court under the act and functions at Delhi. At the state level, consumer court is called **State Consumer Commission**. And at the district level, the court is known as **District Forum** or **District Consumer Court**.
   - The district level court deals with the cases involving claims upto ₹20 lakhs. The state level courts between ₹20 lakhs and ₹1 crore.
   - The national level court deals with cases involving claims exceeding ₹1 crore. If a case is dismissed in district level court, the consumer can also appeal in state and then in national level courts.
   - These courts are required to dispose off each complaint within 90 days.
   - These courts reduce burden on other courts like High Courts, District Courts and the Supreme Court.

At present, there are more than 500 district courts operating in the country.

Consumer Protection Councils

Consumer Protection Councils are formed by a group of people working as a social force. It does not have legal status.

Functions

(i) They guide consumers on how to file cases in the consumer court.
(ii) On many occasions, they also represent individual consumer in the consumer courts.
(iii) They also create awareness among the consumers.

Other Consumer Protection Measures

In order to protect the interest of the consumers, the government adopted three strategies, legislative, administrative and technical. We have already discussed legal measures above. Now, we will mention some other consumer protection measures undertaken by the government as follows.

Administrative Measures

Distributing essential commodities through Public Distribution System (PDS) is an administrative measure. Public distribution system is the system under which foodgrains are procured by the Food Corporation of India (FCI) at pre-announced prices and then distributed through government regulated fair price shops among the poorest section of the society. PDS with a network of 5.5 lakhs fair price shops (also known as ration shops) is perhaps the largest distribution network of its type in the world. It is operated under the joint responsibility of the central and state governments. Apart from ensuring food security to the poor, the PDS is also expected to prevent hoarding, black marketing and over-charging by traders.

Technical Measures

Technical measures consist of standardisation of the products. Standardisation saves the consumers from malpractices. It ensures high quality of product. Under standardisation of products, government lays down the minimum standard for the products. For maintaining these minimum standard, government has created **Bureau of Indian Standards (BIS)** and **Agmark**. The BIS is for industrial and consumer goods, while Agmark is meant for agricultural products. BIS was earlier known as Indian Standards Institution (ISI), whose headquarter is located in New Delhi. It has the responsibility of laying down the standards for industrial and consumer goods on a scientific basis and certifying the goods that meet the standards and the prescribed quality. In case of dissatisfaction with the quality of a certified product, a consumer can complain to the nearest regional office of the BIS.

AGMARK

The grade standards for agricultural goods are notified under the Agricultural Produce (Grading and Marketing) Act, 1937, as amended in 1986. The grade standards for agricultural produce are popularly known as AGMARK.

The Food Safety and Standards Authority of India (FSSAI) also provides a mark which is used to inform customers about quality certification of packaged food products.

Agmark is implemented under the Agricultural Produce **(Grading and Marketing Act, 1937)** as amended in 1986. This scheme is run by the **Directorate of Marketing and Intelligence (DMI)** in the Ministry of Agriculture, Government of India. Products such as honey, ghee and spices carry such market.

DID YOU KNOW

Standardisation of Products

Commodity	Mark	Logo
Industrial goods	ISI	
Agricultural Products	AGMARK	
Packaged Food items	FSSAI	
Gold Jewellery	Hallmark	

Keeping in view the consumer interest, the Government has recently started standards in Gold Jewellery Certification (popularly known as Hallmarking of Gold Jewellery) which was started in April 2000 on a voluntary basis.

International Organisation for Standardisation

The International Organisation for Standardisation (ISO) provides common international standard. The head office of ISO is located in Geneva. The ISO 6000, ISO 9000 or ISO 14,000 indicate specific levels of standard for a particular group of products. The ISO marked goods can be easily sold in the international market.

Duties of a consumer

A good consumer is one who not only knows about his rights but also understands his duties as a consumer. In order to secure the rights, consumers have fulfil the following duties :

(i) While purchasing the goods, consumer should look at the quality of the product as well as on guarantee or warrantee period. Consumer should preferably purchase standardised products which contain seal of ISI or Agmark.

(ii) Consumer should ask for a cash memo and warranty card.

(iii) Consumers must be aware of their rights and duties.

(iv) Consumers should form consumer awareness organisations, which can be given representation in various committees formed by the government and other bodies in the matters relating to the consumers.

(v) Consumers must make complaint for their genuine grievances. They should know the method how to proceed on when cheated.

GLOSSARY

Monopolistic	: Relating to a person or business that has exclusive possession or control of the supply of a commodity or service.
Public Distribution System	: It is a government-sponsored chain of shops entrusted with the work of distributing basic food and non-food commodities to India's poor at subsidised rates.
Standardisation	: The process of developing, promoting and possibly mandating standards-based and compatible technologies and processes within a given industry.
Bureau of Indian Standards (BIS)	: BIS is responsible for the harmonious development of the activities of standardisation, marking and quality certification of goods.
AGMARK	: It is a certification mark employed on agricultural products in India, assuring that they conform to a set of standards approved by the Directorate of Marketing ('Ag' to mean agriculture and 'mark' for a certification mark).
Indian Standards Institution (ISI)	: It was established to create standards for the orderly industrial growth and maintaining quality in industrial production.
Consumer Courts	: Consumer Courts refer to those courts which have been established under Consumer Protection Act, 1986 at district, state and national levels for the protection of consumer interests.

LET'S RECAPITULATE

- Consumer rights refer to the legal rights which are given to the consumers to protect themselves against wrong practices of sellers in the market.
- Right to be informed means the right of information about the quantity and quality of the product.
- In October 2005, the Government of India enacted a law, popularly known as RTI Act, which ensures the citizens all the information about the functioning of government departments.
- Consumer Protection Act (COPRA), was passed by the government in 1986 for the protection of consumer's rights.
- Under COPRA, a consumer has the right to choose the good among a variety of goods which he/she likes.
- Consumers have the right to seek redressal against unfair trade practices and exploitation.
- To protect the interests of consumers, the government adopted three strategies, i.e., legislative, administrative and technical.
- The grade standards for agricultural goods are notified under Agricultural Produce (Grading and Marketing Act, 1937) as amended in 1986.
- Bureau of Indian Standards (BIS) is for industrial and consumer goods, while AGMARK is meant for agricultural produce.
- A good consumer is one who not only knows about his rights but also understands his duties as a consumer.

CHECK YOUR UNDERSTANDING

1. Explain the right to choose as consumer's right.
2. If any damage is done to a consumer by a trader, under which consumer right one can move to consumer court to get compensation.
3. What is meant by consumer right?
4. Write any two rights of consumers?
5. What do you mean by consumer courts?
6. When was the Consumer Protection Act enacted?
7. How do the logo of ISI and Agmark help the consumers?
8. On which products is the ISI mark used?
9. Which logo helps consumers to get assured quality of Jewellery?

EXERCISES

I. A. Multiple Choice Questions

1. Which of the following does not fall under Consumer Rights?
   (a) Right to be informed
   (b) Right to choose
   (c) Right to seek government help
   (d) Right to represent in the consumer courts
2. Which of the following is not a right of consumers? [CBSE 2011]
   (a) Right to Safety
   (b) Right to be Informed
   (c) Right to Choose
   (d) Right to Constitutional Remedies
3. Which one of the following is not true regarding the Right to Safety? [CBSE 2011]
   (a) Right to be protected against unsafe appliances
   (b) Right to be protected against unsafe working conditions
   (c) Right to seek information about functioning of government departments
   (d) Right to be protected against services which are hazardous of life
4. Suppose you want to buy toothpaste and the shop owner says that he/she can sell the toothpaste only if you buy a toothbrush, which of your right is being violated by the shopkeeper? [CBSE 2011]
   (a) Right to Safety (b) Right to be Informed (c) Right to Choose (d) Right to Represent
5. 'Hallmark' is used as a logo for which one of the following? [CBSE 2010, 2013]
   (a) Agriculture products (b) Jewellery (c) Electrical goods (d) Electronic goods
6. ISI mark can be seen on which of the following items? [CBSE 2013]
   (a) Jewellery (b) Edible oil (c) Electrical appliances (d) Cereals
7. On which of the following products Agmark is used? [CBSE 2011]
   (a) Certification of edible oil and cereals
   (b) Certification maintained for standardisation of jewellery
   (c) Certification of electronic items
   (d) Certification of LPG cylinders
8. Which one of the following is the agency that develops standards for goods and services in India? [CBSE 2011]
   (a) COPRA
   (b) National Consumer Court
   (c) Consumer Protection Councils
   (d) Bureau of Indian Standard
9. On which of the following date do we celebrate the National Consumer Day? [CBSE 2011]
   (a) 24 October (b) 14 October (c) 24 December (d) 14 December
10. The 'World Consumer Right Day' is celebrated on *[CBSE 2011]*
    (a) May 15 (b) July 27 (c) March 15 (d) October 2

B. Match the following items given in Column A with those in Column B. Choose the correct answer from the options given below.

1.

	Column A		Column B
A.	A way of consumer exploitation	(i)	High prices
B.	Mixing inferior quality products with superior products	(ii)	1986
C.	Consumer Protection Act	(iii)	Adulteration
D.	National Consumer Day in India	(iv)	24th December

Mark the correct option.

(a) (i) – (iii) – (ii) – (iv)
(b) (iv) – (i) – (iii) – (ii)
(c) (i) – (ii) – (iii) – (iv)
(d) (iv) – (iii) – (ii) – (i)

2.

	Column A		Column B
A.	Grade for agricultural products	(i)	ISI
B.	Grade for Jewellery	(ii)	ISO
C.	Grade for industrial and consumer goods	(iii)	AGMARK
D.	Grade for international standard	(iv)	Hallmark

Mark the correct option.

(a) (ii) – (i) – (iv) – (iii)
(b) (iii) – (iv) – (ii) – (i)
(c) (ii) – (iii) – (i) – (iv)
(d) (iii) – (iv) – (i) – (ii)

C. Fill in the blanks.

1. Adulteration is ______________ to health.
2. When sellers deceive innocent customers by giving artificial articles in the name of original one, it is called ______________.
3. Sometimes consumers are exploited by the sellers by selling ______________ goods.
4. The standard mark given to industrial product by BIS is ______________.
5. The standard mark given to Desi Ghee is ______________.
6. National Consumer Day is celebrated on ______________.
7. ______________ guide the consumers on how to file the cases in the consumer court.

II. A. Very short answer type questions.

1. Who is a consumer?
2. What is consumer protection? [CBSE 2009]
3. What does COPRA stand for? [CBSE 2009]
4. When did Consumer Protection Act come into effect?
5. Which day is celebrated as National Consumer Day? [CBSE 2009]
6. What is adulteration? [CBSE 2015]
7. What is food adulteration? Give two examples of food adulteration.
8. Name two standardisation marks used in India as a certificate of quality.
9. What mark would you look for on a packet of bread?
10. Which sign shows the quality of gold jewellery?
11. What should be done by the Government to save the people from being exploited?
12. When is the World Consumer Day celebrated?
13. Name the organisation which provides certification of standardisation for industrial products in India.
14. Name the organisation which provides certification of standardisation for agricultural goods.
15. Suppose your parents want to purchase gold jewellery along with you, then which logo will you look for on the jewellery? [CBSE 2015]
16. How do the logos of ISI, Agmark and Hallmark help the consumers? [CBSE 2016]
17. Why was the Consumer Protection Act enabled by the Indian Parliament? [CBSE 2015]

B. Short Answer Type Questions.

1. Give any three salient features of Consumer Protection Act, 1986.
2. What are the rights of consumers? Mention any three.
3. What are the important duties of consumers? Mention any three.
4. Explain how the government of India protects the interests of the consumers by standardisation of products. What is the need for consumer awareness?
5. Explain the 'Right to be Informed' as a consumer right. [CBSE 2013]

6. How is the consumer redressal process becoming cumbersome? Give four reasons? [CBSE 2012]
7. Describe any two features of 'Right to Safety' as consumer right. [CBSE 2012, 2016]
8. Explain the Right to be Informed as a consumer right. [CBSE 2013]

   OR

   Explain with suitable examples the meaning of Right to be Informed as provided under Consumer Protection Act, 1986. [CBSE 2008]
9. Explain 'Right to Choose' with an example. [CBSE 2013]
10. What is CORPA? When was it introduced? [CBSE 2016]

C. Long Answer Type Questions.

1. Write a note on Consumer Movement in India.
2. Why are rules and regulations required in the market place? Give three reasons. [CBSE 2011, 2013]

   OR

   Describe the conditions in which markets do not work in a fair manner. [CBSE 2015]
3. Why is protection required in the market place?
4. What are the various ways in which a consumer is exploited in India?
5. Mention the factors responsible for consumers' exploitation in India.
6. Write four salient features of Consumer Protection Act, 1986?
7. What are the rights of consumers according to the Consumer Protection Act, 1986?
8. What are the duties of a consumer?
9. What legal measures were taken by the government to strengthen the consumers in India?
10. "Limited competition and limited information result in the exploitation of consumers." Do you agree with this statement? If yes, give two arguments in support of your answer.
11. Describe the conditions on which markets do not work in a fair manner. [CBSE 2015]
12. Explain any two rights of a consumer. [CBSE 2017]
13. How did consumer movement arise in India? Explain. [CBSE 2009, 2011]

    OR

    The consumer movement arose out of dissatisfaction of the consumers. Justify the statement with arguments. [CBSE 2013, 2016]
14. Why was Consumer Protection Act enacted by the Indian Parliament? [CBSE 2015]
15. Mention any four duties of a good consumer? [CBSE 2012, 2016]
16. How do Consumer Protection Councils help consumers? Explain three ways. [CBSE 2012]
17. Describe the provisions made under Consumer Protection Act 1986 for redressal of consumer disputes? [CBSE 2013, 2016, 2017]

ANSWERS

MCQS

1. (c) 2. (d) 3. (c) 4. (c) 5. (b) 6. (c) 7. (a) 8. (d)
9. (c) 10. (c)

Fill in the blanks.

1. injurious 2. deception 3. sub-standard 4. ISI
5. AGMARK 6. 24th December 7. Consumer protection councils